PERIOD-STYLE
SOFT FURNISHINGS

PERIOD-STYLE
SOFT FURNISHINGS

JUDITH MILLER

PHOTOGRAPHY BY JAMES MERRELL

MITCHELL BEAZLEY

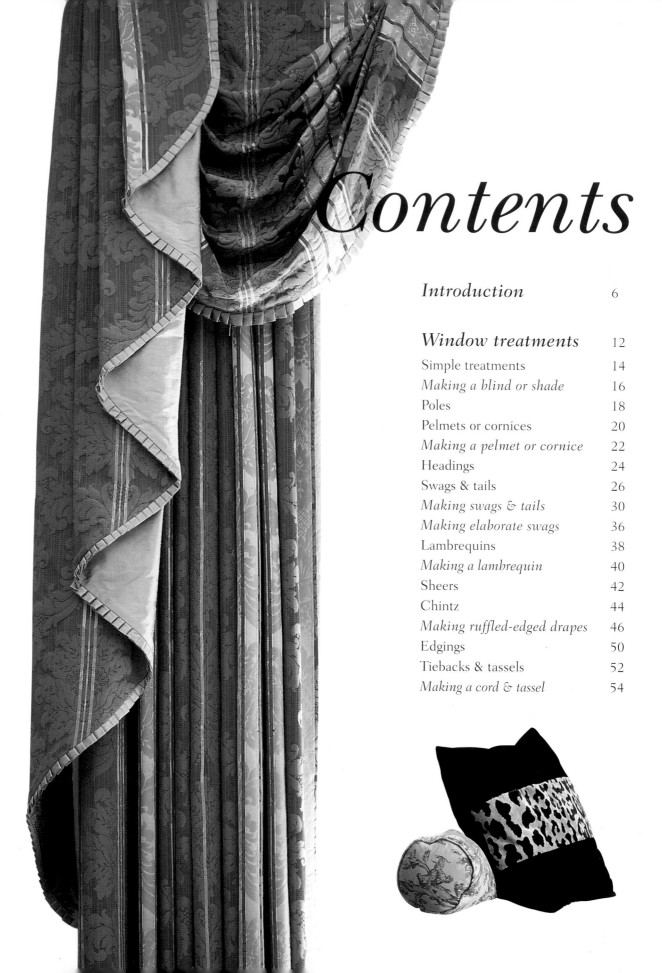

First published in Great Britain in 1996
by Mitchell Beazley an imprint of
Reed Consumer Books Limited
Michelin House
81 Fulham Road
London SW3 6RB
and Auckland, Melbourne, Singapore
and Toronto

Chief Contributor **John Wainwright**
Photography **James Merrell**
Colour Illustrations **Claire Davies**
Projects **Diana Lodge**

Editor **Nina Sharman**
Art Editor **Rozelle Bentheim, Emma Boys**
Designer **Adam Hays**
Production **Juliet Butler, Christina Quigley**

Executive Editor **Judith More**
Art Director **Gaye Allen**
Executive Art Editor **Janis Utton**

Endpaper fabric **The Gainsborough Silk
Weaving Company Limited**

A CIP record for this book is available from
the British Library

ISBN 1 85732 792 6

The publishers have made every effort to
ensure that all instructions given in this book
are accurate and safe, but they cannot accept
liability for any resulting injury, damage or loss
to either person or property whether direct or
consequential and howsoever arising.

Produced by Mandarin Offset
Printed and bound in China

Contents

Introduction   6

Window treatments   12
Simple treatments   14
Making a blind or shade   16
Poles   18
Pelmets or cornices   20
Making a pelmet or cornice   22
Headings   24
Swags & tails   26
Making swags & tails   30
Making elaborate swags   36
Lambrequins   38
Making a lambrequin   40
Sheers   42
Chintz   44
Making ruffled-edged drapes   46
Edgings   50
Tiebacks & tassels   52
Making a cord & tassel   54

Floor, wall &
door treatments   56

Formal rugs & carpets   58

Country rugs   62

Making a rag rug   64

Wall treatments   66

How to cover walls in fabric   70

Door curtains   72

Upholstery   74

Tapestry   76

Damask & silk   80

Making squabs for a day bed   84

Checks & stripes   88

Velvets & leather   90

Upholstery styles   92

Making loose covers   94

Buttoned treatments   98

Bed treatments   100

Four-posters   102

Dressing a four-poster   112

Half-testers   114

Creating a half-tester   116

Corona style   120

Making a corona   122

Standard beds   126

Quilts   130

Accessories   132

Table linen   134

Decorative tablecloths   136

Cushions   138

Decorative details   142

Basic techniques   146

The sample book   151

Directory   167

Glossary   171

Index   175

Acknowledgments   176

Introduction

Before the 20th-century invention of man-made fibres, furnishing fabrics were produced from silk, wool, linen or cotton and coloured mainly by vegetable or mineral dyes. Synthetic dyes have been available only since the mid-19th century. Patterns and textures were created by weaving, embroidery, hand-painting or printing. Raw fibres, manufactured goods, patterns and motifs, as well as methods of production, were being traded extensively between countries and across continents.

Medieval and Renaissance silks

Prior to AD 552, when two Byzantine monks smuggled silkworm eggs out of China in bamboo canes, the West was dependent on Chinese exports for raw silk and silk textiles. Thereafter, however, European sericulture and silk-weaving began developing in earnest and dependence on the East lessened.

During the Middle Ages, Constantinople produced elaborately patterned silks on drawlooms and then exported them to Europe via Italy. Finely patterned silk velvets were also made in Spain. During the Renaissance, the Italian cities of Palermo, Lucca, Florence, Venice, Genoa, Bologna and Milan made a wide range of wonderful heavy brocades, patterned velvets, damasks, satins, taffetas, and silk trimmings. Lyons, in France, also became a leading centre for silk-weaving.

Left: *A Duncan Phyfe mahogany sofa c.1835, covered in Scalamandré documentary red and gold lampas.*

Medieval and Renaissance woollens

Typical woven woollen cloths of the period included worsteds (such as say and fustian) and camlet – the latter prized for the softness of its angora wool (imported from the Near East). Most of the wool produced during this period originated in England, although Burgundy and Spain were also leading exporters. The main weaving centres were in England, Italy and the

Low Countries. Flemish woollen weaving declined in the early 15th century but it was replaced by a thriving linen-based industry – linen damasks became their most popular product and became a substantial European export.

Opus Anglicanum

English embroidery or needlework ("Opus Anglicanum") was highly prized in Medieval Europe. Embroidered tapestries, worked in silk, wool and gold thread on linen or velvet grounds, were widely used in wealthier households. As English needlework declined during the 14th century, the Low Countries, Burgundy and Florence became pre-eminent in this field.

17th-century expansion

The European textile industry expanded during the 17th century, following a rise in living standards and a greater emphasis on luxury and comfort. This was most evident at Louis XIV's Palace of Versailles, where the lavishly furnished interiors set fashions for the rest of Europe. The opening of links with India and China, and increased trade following the formation of the English, French and Dutch East India Companies, further fuelled supply and demand – as did the foundation of American colonies.

Indiennes

At the end of the 16th century, the first cotton *indiennes* (or chintzes) were imported to France from India. These brightly coloured, hand-blocked and hand-painted calicoes were

Above: *A hand-stitched, 19th-century, paisley-pattern quilt, on top of a 19th-century French "boutie". The fashion for quilting in America, Britain and France was primarily a domestic rather than a commercial activity.*

colourfast (and washable). They became highly popular by the late 17th century, posing a serious threat to the wool and silk industries. European governments imposed severe restrictions on their importation and these were not lifted until 1720 in England and 1759 in France. Sanctions were also imposed on European copies of chintzes, although English manufacturers were allowed to export to American colonies.

17th-century silk, wool and linen

The addition of a bobbin to the spinning wheel, and a more sophisticated use of the drawboy loom, resulted in numerous "new draperies" during the 17th century. Silk damasks and plain, ribbed, watered, brocaded and taffeta silks were produced in quantity, particularly by the French Huguenot refugees who settled in London and the north of England, while Genoa in Italy and Lyons in France made high-quality, boldly patterned velvets. *Gaufrage* velvets were also extremely popular, as was brocatelle. Raw and finished silks were also imported into Europe from China.

Large quantities of loose-linen chair covers and bed and table linen were made throughout Europe. Linen and woollen damasks were highly fashionable and less expensive than silk equivalents. Also, for the first time on any scale in Europe, wool was used to make woven and embroidered carpets. These began as turkey work copies of Persian and Turkish imports, but at Savonnerie in France, European-style patterns and motifs were introduced.

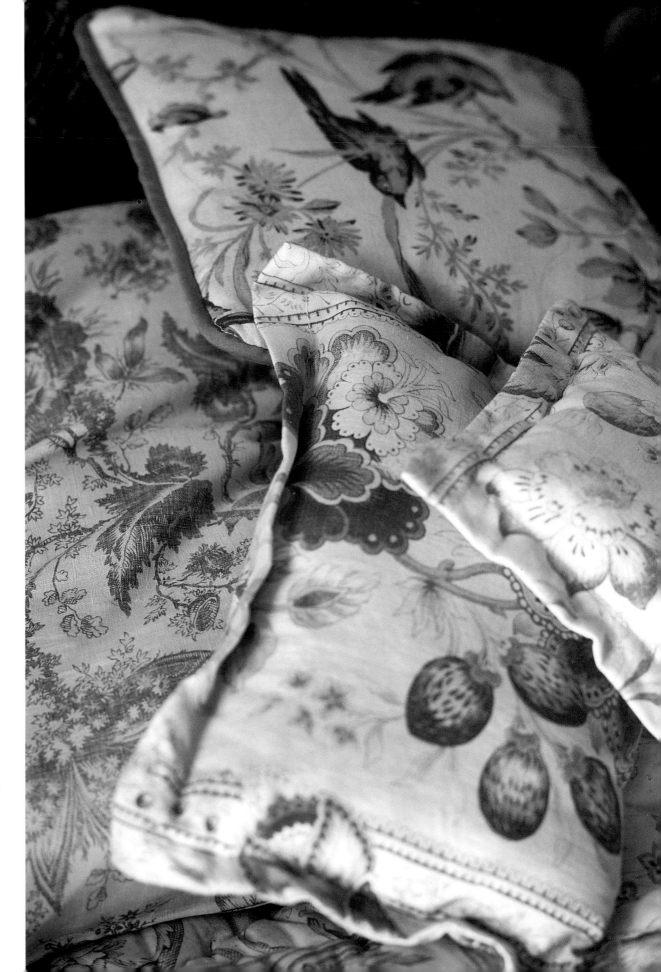

17th-century needlework and lace

Crewelwork cushions or pillows were fashionable during the 17th century, while petit-point needlework was used for seat covers. Stumpwork was used for panel pictures and the decoration of mirrors. Flemish bobbin lace, from Brussels, Mechlin and Antwerp, was in demand from the 1550s through to the 1690s, while the Italian cities of Venice, Genoa and Milan became main centres for needlepoint lace. However, from the mid-17th century, French lace from Paris, Alençon and Argenton became increasingly fashionable in Europe and America, despite import restrictions.

Early to mid-18th century

Although textile production flourished during the first half of the 18th century, international trade and the movement of skilled labour was often inhibited by governments protecting their home industries. However, there were ways around this and the smuggling of lace and silk became widespread. In the 1740s, Lord Wilton was said to have imported French carpet weavers into England hidden in wine barrels.

The silk industry prospered as the manufacture of window-, bed- and wall-hangings, and upholstered furniture, increased. Lyons in France and Spitalfields in England led the way,

Right: *A collection of 18th- and 19th-century toile-covered cushions. Hand-blocked and machine-printed chintzes were tremendously fashionable from the last quarter of the 18th century through to the 1890s.*

with much of their product exported to America. For the less wealthy, woollen stuffs, moreen and harateen provided alternatives.

The production of woollen carpets also increased – notably at Savonnerie and Aubusson in France along with Kidderminster, Wilton and Axminster in England. Linen cloths for tables, beds and linings were much in demand. Cotton chintzes, although highly sought after, were difficult to obtain in Europe and America – largely because of continuing government restrictions.

The Industrial Revolution

The period from 1750 to 1880 witnessed major innovations, and rapidly expanding markets and manufacturing output. The concept of interior design emerged and was conveyed to the new middle classes in England and America via publications such as *Ackermann's Repository of Arts* (1809–28) and Thomas Hope's *Household Furniture and Interior Decoration* (1807).

Technological advances were numerous and included spinning machines (1764–9), steam and horse-powered looms (1785–93), the automated Jacquard loom (1805), the dobby loom (1824), a velvet-pile carpeting-machine (1851), lace-making machines (1812–3), mechanized embroidery machines and the sewing machines of the 1850s.

Parallel advances included the development of engraved copper-plate printing (1752),

Left: *Detail of a Victorian beadwork firescreen, in an early 19th-century American mansion.*

and water- and steam-powered roller-printing (1783). Improved dyeing techniques were developed during the early 19th century, and the arrival of synthetic aniline dyes in the 1850s widened the palette of colours available.

19th-century cottons, silks and woollens

As a result of these technological advances cotton gradually superseded silk as the most fashionable fabric. Vast quantities of printed, and often glazed, pictorial and floral toiles (chintzes) were produced from 1770 onward. *Toiles de Jouy* (in France) were the most famous – although Paris, Rouen, Nantes, Bordeaux, Marseilles, Provence, London and Philadelphia were also home to key manufacturers. Cotton checks and stripes were also increasingly used for furnishings, and muslin was widely employed for sheers and drapes.

However, silk furnishings remained fashionable, with the new looms of Genoa in Italy, Lyons in France and Spitalfields in England, weaving complex and elaborately patterned damasks and velvets well suited to grander interiors. Similarly, small-patterned wool damasks and moreens, produced on Jacquard looms, were competitively priced against cotton and produced in quantity.

Pre-industrial traditions

Machine-made lace covered numerous surfaces in the average Victorian home. In many respects, it represented the Industrial Revolution's triumph of machine over man. However, a

return to traditional methods of production was encouraged by the 19th-century Aesthetic and Arts and Crafts Movements. This was reflected in the revivals of Opus Anglicanum in Britain as well as beadwork, crochet and quilting in the United States. It is echoed again today in the numerous documentary fabrics dating from the 17th century onward which are available from specialist manufacturers and suppliers.

Right: *Scalamandré documentary white mull drapes, secured with mid-19th-century gilt metal and white glass floral-shaped tie-backs.*

Below: *19th-century, machine-made lace.*

Window treatments

In her highly influential book *The Decoration of Houses*, published in 1898, the American writer Edith Wharton suggested that better houses had less need for drapery. In her view, many window treatments upset the architectural symmetry of windows, often spoiling a good view. While this can be seen as an understandable reaction to some of the excesses of the later Victorian era, it ignores the fact that the vast majority of window drapery since the 17th century has added architectural interest to interiors, and provided colour, texture, comfort and style. Indeed, it has more often than not hidden a multitude of sins.

Above & Right: *A reception room at the Calhoun Mansion, in Charleston, South Carolina, USA. The reproduction 19th-century drapes are made of watered silk, with floral damask tails, deep fringing and tasselling. The original gilt poles are from the 1870s. The ensemble reflects the status of both the house and the owners.*

Simple treatments

Up until the mid-17th century, wooden shutters were commonly used at windows and drapes were something of a rarity. Where used in England, drapes were made of a single piece of material which could be pulled to one side and was suspended by tapes or rings on an iron rod. French and Italian drapes were slightly more elaborate, and often hung in pairs which could be pulled to either side. Typical fabrics included sarsenet in grander houses and worsted wool in more modest dwellings – while velvet and brocade was used in Italy and France.

From the second half of the 17th century onward, window treatments in larger houses became more sophisticated. Lambrequins, pelmets or cornices, swags-and-tails and tie-backs were employed, as were a wide range of elaborately patterned woven or printed fabrics, often embellished with *passementerie*.

In more modest country dwellings in both Europe and America the simpler treatments of the 15th and 16th centuries remained fashionable, and have remained so to the present day. In the cities and towns it was not until the last quarter of the 19th century that the simpler approach came back into vogue. This was partly a reaction to some of the overly draped and gloomy Victorian interiors – and partly a belief that elaborate heavy drapes were dust traps and therefore unhealthy.

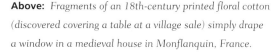

Above: *Fragments of an 18th-century printed floral cotton (discovered covering a table at a village sale) simply drape a window in a medieval house in Monflanquin, France.*

Far left: *An inexpensive modern French cotton fabric with a stylized floral pattern is "puddled" on the floor below a window in a 17th-century château on the Dordogne, France.*

Left: *An 18th-century toile window pelmet or valance from the same château. It may have been used originally as part of a pelmet or cornice on a four-poster or half-tester bed.*

Right: *Modern cotton window drapes based on the traditional Perigord check appear at the Château du Parc in the Dordogne, France. The armchair is draped with a hand-embroidered sheet, while the stool in front of it is covered with a piece of 19th-century hand-stitched quilting.*

Making a blind or shade

Above: *This toile de Jouy blind or shade complements French pleated curtains with furbelows, making an extremely elegant window treatment.*

MATERIALS

- ◆ Basic sewing kit (see page 146)
- ◆ Main fabric
- ◆ Lining fabric
- ◆ Ringed or looped tape – for each edge of the blind and at intervals of 15–20cm (6–8in) across the blind
- ◆ Nylon cord – same amount as tape above plus enough to go across the top of the blind and for the side cords
- ◆ Wooden battens, one 5 x 2.5cm (2 x 1in), measuring the width of the blind, and one 2.5cm (1in) wide for the bottom hem
- ◆ Brackets with screws, tacks, screw eyes
- ◆ Cleat hook with fixing screws

A Roman blind or shade has a restrained elegance that complements a lavish, full curtain treatment. The folds are formed by rows of ringed or looped tape at the back of the blind, with nylon cord threaded vertically through them. In the past, the rings and tape were bought separately, but today it is simpler to buy ready-ringed or looped tape that sets the size of the pleats. If you require pleats of a different depth machine-stitch plain tapes down the back of the blind and sew on small curtain rings by hand. The blind is usually tacked to a wooden batten which can be attached with brackets to the underside of the top reveal of the window, and positioned so as to leave a gap between the blind and the curtains in front of it. Alternatively the batten can be attached outside the reveal or window frame, supported by brackets fixed to the wall. Choose a good-quality fabric, and if patterned make sure that the pattern has been accurately printed along the grain lines, otherwise your blind may either look or hang out of true.

1 For blinds inside the reveal, measure the height of the window and add 15cm (6in) for top and bottom hems, and the width plus 7.5cm (3in) for side hems. For blinds outside the reveal measure the chosen height (above and below the window) and the width plus hems. If you need to join fabric together to gain the correct width, have a central panel with two smaller sections on either side and make extra allowances for seams and pattern repeats (see pages 149–50). You will need the same amount of lining material as main fabric. Cut out the main and lining fabric to the above dimensions, making the lining 5cm (2in) narrower.

2 If necessary, using plain seams, join widths of main fabric together; join the lining in the same way. Place the lining on top of the main fabric, with right sides facing. Pin and machine-stitch side seams, taking a 1.5cm (⅝in) seam allowance. Turn right side out and press, so the seamlines run down the wrong side, 2.5cm (1in) in from each side edge.

3 At the bottom edge, turn the main fabric and lining over 1cm (⅜in) to the lining side and then a further 10cm (4in). Press the hem and then pin close to the folded edge.

4 Making sure that the rings or loops align horizontally, pin the tape down the length of the blind. Start by covering the two side seams, and then set the tape at evenly spaced intervals of approximately 15–20cm (6–8in) across the width of the blind (the closer the lengths of tape are placed the more tailored the folds will be). The lowest row of rings or loops should lie just above the folded and pinned hem. Tuck the ends of tape under the pinned hem at the lower edge.

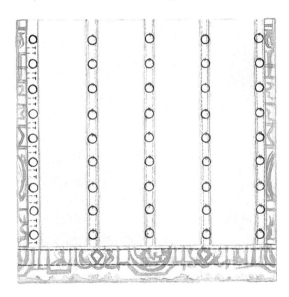

5 When you are satisfied that all the tapes are in the correct position, machine-stitch across the lower hem, close to the folded edge. Stitch a second, parallel line, 3cm (¼in) below the first, making a casing for the batten. Next, using the zipper foot of your machine, stitch down each side of each length of tape, stitching through both layers of fabric and stopping at the hem stitching line.

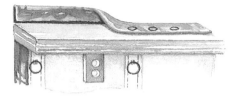

6 Turn over 2.5cm (1in) at the top edge of the blind; press and machine-stitch in place. Screw the brackets to the batten. Attach the blind to the batten with tacks spaced at approximately 10cm (4in) intervals along the top edge.

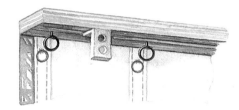

7 On the underside of the batten, place screw eyes in the wood to correspond with each row of ringed or looped tape.

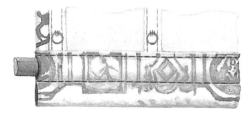

8 Slide the wooden lath into the hem casing (it should be marginally shorter than the casing) and slipstitch the side edges closed to hold it in place. Secure the cleat hook at a convenient height at the side of the window from which you wish to pull up the blind.

9 Cut a sufficient length of cord to be tied to the bottom ring or loop on the first row (the side opposite to the cleat hook), and then threaded up through each ring or loop, across the top through the screw eyes, and down the length of the blind at the cleat hook side. Repeat this process, tying lengths of cord to each bottom ring or loop and threading through the rings or loops on each row of tape and across the top, always leaving sufficient cord to hang down the side to loop around the cleat hook.

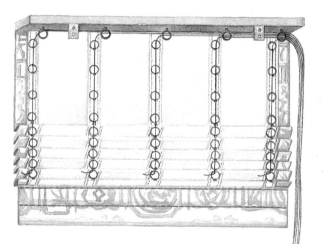

10 Fix the batten in position, either securing it inside or outside the reveal. (If the ends of the batten are visible, they can be covered with spare fabric or painted.) With the blind down, check that all cords are at an even tension, and then tie the ends together. To raise the blind, pull all the cords together and wind them in a figure-of-eight around the cleat hook. At first you will need to smooth the pleats into place, making sure that they are even. After a few days the folds will form automatically when the blind is drawn up.

Poles

During the 17th century, drapes were suspended from iron or horn rings on iron rods attached to the wall. This remained the case until the 1770s, although the rods were masked with a pelmet or cornice for much of the 18th century. While cord-and-pulley "French rods" still required a pelmet or cornice to hide the workings, rods came back on display in Empire, Regency and Federal interiors. Layered window treatments were invariably hung from decorative poles made of brass or gilded, lacquered or painted wood. Often ribbed or reeded, these were embellished with elaborate finials, brackets and rosettes – Egyptian, Chinoiserie, and Classical Roman and Greek motifs providing inspiration. During the Victorian era, pelmets or cornices were reintroduced – with any rods showing being over-ornamented. However, by the 20th century plainer and slimmer rods found favour again.

Above: Poles and drapes in 1830s Greek-revival style, at the Old Merchant's House, New York, USA.

Above & Below left: Brass rods and poles were generally favoured in the grand salons of townhouses, while wooden ones were used in lesser rooms and country homes.

Right: Understated poles can be employed to enhance the fabric used for the drapes, as with this "aged" chintz, by Bennison, in a manoir in Luzech, France.

Far left: Simple brass rods and heavy, wild-silk drapes lend classical elegance to a reception room in an 1830s Greek-revival townhouse, in Charleston, South Carolina, USA.

Pelmets or cornices

In 16th-century France, shaped, pleated and fringed pelmets or cornices were fixed above windows – a practice that gradually extended to England during the 17th century. During the latter part of this period, pelmets or cornices became more elaborate and were typified in the Baroque designs of Daniel Marot. His festooned pull-up drapes were topped by complex pelmets or cornices either stiffened, shaped and trimmed with tassels or gathered in pleats secured by rosettes and falling into swags and tails.

During the first half of the 18th century, the workings of pull-up curtains were hidden by a pelmet or cornice. Curtains were invariably topped with elegantly shaped and stiffened pelmets or cornices embellished with appliqué or embroidery. By the 1750s, pelmets or cornices had softened, and were designed as shallow swags with small tails and bells, which were often combined with festooned silk drapes. It was not unusual to find the Venetian windows of Palladian mansions dressed with curved pelmet or cornice boards in the middle (for the swags) and straight boards at the sides (for the tails).

In the latter part of the 18th century, the elaboration of pelmets or cornices intensified. Sheraton designed Gothic-style versions with narrow "pagoda-style" cornices above. In France they were often castellated, and there was an increased use of borders, braids, ribbons, bows and tassels. In America, fashionable designs were copied from European pattern books.

In early 19th-century Regency, French Restoration and later Federal interiors, drapes tended to be hung from elaborate poles, and pelmets or cornices went out of fashion. However, they were sometimes still used to link windows on the same wall.

During the Victorian age the pelmet or cornice reappeared, initially in the form of the lambrequin – a flat, shaped pelmet or cornice which reached down the sides of the window. Traditional pelmets or cornices were also used and were fashioned in a variety of revival styles. Some were also built out in a semi-circular or rectangular shape and covered with goblet pleating, and others were augmented above with stamped brass or gilded wood cornices.

Above left: *A gilded wooden cornice with "old gold" silk damask fabric, in the hall of a late 18th-century townhouse in Charleston, South Carolina, USA.*

Far left: *The simple window treatment in an 1830s house in Galena, Illinois, USA, is reminiscent of the purely decorative drapes of the earlier Federal period.*

Left: *Reproduction, mahogany brass-mounted cornices, valances of documentary, striped-crimson moiré silk with cording by Scalamandré, 19th-century tassels and gilt-metal tie-backs, Andrew Low House, Savannah, Georgia, USA.*

Right: *The pelmet or cornice in the parlour of Andrew Low House, Georgia, USA, is Scalamandré documentary lampas. The undercurtains are embroidered Swiss-cotton eyelet.*

Top: *The library pelmet or cornice in the Melrose Mansion, Natchez, Mississippi, USA, is a pastiche of an 1830s design.*

Above: *Wild-silk pelmets or cornices in the General Walter Gresham bedroom at Rosalie in Natchez, USA.*

Making a pelmet or cornice

Above: *The relatively simple design of this fabric pelmet or cornice is enhanced by sides that are folded back, tasseled trumpets and fringing.*

MATERIALS

◆ Basic sewing kit (see page 146)
◆ Wall lining paper and pencil
◆ Brocade or other suitable fabric
◆ Lining fabric
◆ Interlining
◆ Bullion fringing
◆ Two matching tassels
◆ Two matching rosettes
◆ Small brass rings and hooks, tacks, or touch-and-close tape
◆ Wooden moulding or pelmet board and angle brackets

Made from a rich brocade and trimmed with a heavy bullion fringe in Victorian style, this gently curved fabric pelmet or cornice is fitted under a piece of wooden moulding with a distressed gilded finish. It is an attractive window dressing in itself, but if you wish to screen the window, the pelmet or cornice could conceal a matching roller blind or shade. At its maximum depth in the middle of the window, the pelmet or cornice (excluding the moulding) is in a proportion of one to three with the remaining exposed window below, with the sides falling slightly below this level. Instead of buckram, which would be too stiff for the folded sides, the pelmet or cornice is stiffened with interlining.

Unless you are an experienced woodworker it is advisable to find someone to make the wooden cornice for you. You can finish the moulding by painting or staining it to complement the fabric. Support the moulding with angle brackets placed at each end. This type of fabric pelmet or cornice can also be fitted to a plain board like the one used for the lambrequin featured on page 40 and a heavy braid or cord used to trim the edge.

1 Make a pattern for the pelmet or cornice as above, using lining paper. Measure the width of the moulding, including the returns. Decide on how deep you wish the front curve to fall, how high you wish the rise at either side to be and where you would like the side edges to fall. Join these points together in a gentle curve. At the sides the fabric is doubled back on itself, making three layers in total. Allowing 4cm (1½in) for the top edge that lies behind the cornice, draw one half of the pattern, from the middle of the window (you will then cut it on a fold to make a complete pelmet or cornice). The best way to get the shape for your particular window is to experiment by cutting out a full-scale pattern from paper or old sheeting and pinning it in place. You can then make adjustments to the design in situ.

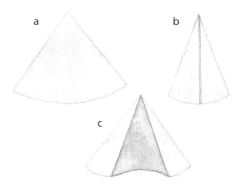

2   Next make a paper pattern for the trumpets. Draw a triangle measuring the finished depth and twice the finished width of the trumpet, giving the lower edge a shallow curve (a). Cut out this shape and then fold the paper so that the two straight edges meet down the middle (b). Flatten the cone, then shape the front edge into a shallow upward curve between the folds (c).

3   Adding 1.5cm (⅝in) seam allowances all around, cut out the pelmet or cornice shape from both main and lining fabrics. Cut out the interlining without seam allowances. Use the trumpet pattern to cut out two each from main fabric, interlining and lining, again adding 1.5cm (⅝in) seam allowances all around.

4   Lockstitch the pelmet or cornice interlining to the back of the main fabric (see page 49). Press and baste the seam allowance over the interlining to the wrong side all around. Along the lower curved edge, make cuts almost up to the seam allowance on upward curves and take notches from the fabric on downward curves, so that you get a smooth foldline. Stitch the fringing in position on the right side of the pelmet or cornice, all along the lower edge.

5   Turn in the seam allowance to the wrong side all around the lining section of the pelmet or cornice, making cuts and notches as necessary; press and baste. Place the lining over the main section wrong sides together and slipstitch around the side edges and along the bottom. Machine-stitch through all thicknesses along the top, close to the folded edges.

6   Fold the sides over three times until you are satisfied with the result. Pin them in place, then, overstitch the top edges, stitching through all layers, to hold the folds in place.

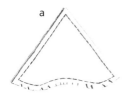

7   To make a trumpet, lay the interlining on the wrong side of the main fabric and baste in place on the seam line around the three sides (a). Press and baste the seam allowance to the wrong side along the curved edge, making cuts up to the seam allowance and taking notches from the fabric as necessary to achieve a smooth finish. Next stitch fringing to the right side of the fabric (b), stopping and starting at the side seamlines (not the raw edges).

8   With right sides together, pin and machine-stitch the two straight edges together, forming a cone. Trim the interlining almost back to the stitching line and cut away the surplus seam allowance at the top, as shown. Press the seam open, and turn the trumpet right side out. With right sides together, stitch the two straight edges of the lining section together. Trim the top corners, as with the main fabric, and press the seam open, then press under the seam allowance all around the lower edge. With wrong sides facing, seams together, push the lining section up into the cone, and slipstitch it in place around the lower edge.

9   Place the trumpet in position on the pelmet or cornice and hand-stitch in place across the top. Attach a rosette (or an upholstery button) with slipstitch to cover the top. Catchstitch the centre back of the trumpet to the pelmet at the lower edge. Hand-stitch a tassel in place so that it hangs down from the inside of the trumpet. Repeat steps 8–10 to make and position the second trumpet.

10   Attach the pelmet or cornice to the back of the moulding with upholstery tacks. Alternatively, stitch small rings to the top of the pelmet or cornice and hang it on hooks or nails fixed in the back of the moulding; or stitch the hooked side of touch-and-close tape along the top edge of the pelmet or cornice and glue the opposite side to the back of the moulding. (If you have used the type of board used for the lambrequin, refer to page 40.)

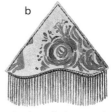

Left & Below: *Having carefully restored the original 18th-century pelmets or cornices, using as much of the surviving fabric as it was possible to save, the owners of this modernized 1795 townhouse, in Charleston, South Carolina, USA, found a modern co-ordinating silk fabric for the drapes. The latter have been edged with rich tasselled braid.*

Above: *The documentary fabrics and wallpapers used at The Burn, a Greek-revival house built in Natchez, Mississippi, USA, in 1832, are by Schumacher and are taken from original samples in their Historic Natchez Collection. The pelmet or cornice is a modern copy of a period original.*

Headings

During the 19th century, it became fashionable to use specific types of heading to produce regular pleating in drapes. For example, cased headings enclosed all but the finials of the rod, and were mainly used to hang tie-back muslin and lace sheers – while French- (pinch-) pleat headings produced tight folds in draw-curtains.

Goblet-pleat headings were formed in the same way as the French pleat, but incorporated small "cups" across the top of the drapes. These were padded, bordered with contrasting fabric for extra definition, and were often repeated on a pelmet or cornice. A popular variation of this, known as a Flemish heading, involved linking the bases of the goblets with cord, either stitched straight across or looped in-between.

Smocked headings were also used by the Victorians, usually to complement architectural fixtures and fittings, like acanthus-leaf mouldings on a cornice above the window.

Right: *A loosely pleated, gathered heading has been used on this valance. The fabric is by Bennison.*

Below: *Goblet pleats were introduced in the 19th century.*

Above & Right: *Elegant valances with hand-sewn smocked headings, in the bedroom of a Norfolk manor house, England.*

Swags & tails

A Classical motif, swags were first incorporated into window treatments in the 17th century, notably by Daniel Marot. Many of his designs included drapes pulled up by a cord to hang in festoons or swags. Similar pull-up, swagged drapes remained fashionable until the middle of the 18th century, particularly in houses with Venetian, or tall, narrow sash windows. Where pelmets or cornices were used, these, too, were often embellished with shallow swagging.

In the Neo-classical interiors of the second half of the 18th century, window treatments became even more formal and opulent, with draped arrangements most popular. Even the simplest examples had swags at each side, with both swags and tails often lined with a contrasting material. "Irregular" drapery was also in vogue, with swags fixed at different heights to form an arch-like effect over the window, as were reefed ("Italian-strung") drapes, which were pulled up and apart by diagonally strung cords to form swags and tails.

Swags could also be used as an additional embellishment to cornices and paired drapes. When swags were used with drapes they appeared to be part of the drapes, but were actually attached to the cornice. Where cornices

and valances were used, they were often softened with attachments of small swags and mini-tails.

Swags abounded in the layered window treatments hung from poles in Regency, Empire and later Federal interiors. Draped headings above the main drapes often incorporated swags or festoons, their pinning hidden behind discs, rosettes and other Classical motifs.

Swags and tails remained a popular feature of drapes and pelmets or cornices in many revival-style window treatments during the rest of the 19th century. They were particularly prevalent in drawing-rooms, where the main drapes were often tied dress curtains.

Right: *The swags and tails of the drapes are echoed in the cornice above in this 1830s American interior.*

Below far right: *An 18th-century style window treatment with swags and tails embracing a central trumpet.*

Left : *An elaborate swagged-and-tailed pelmet or cornice, with deep fringing, and a swagged muslin pull-up blind, in a classic William and Mary, English country house.*

Right & Middle: *Swagged linen drapes with a tapestry border, by Belinda Coote.*

27

Left: *Swagged silk drapes, trimmed with deep bullion fringing and centrally hung tassels, exude opulence in a late 18th-century townhouse in London, England. The window treatment is set against a hand-painted Regency stripe on the walls.*

Right: *A swagged window treatment fashionable during the early 19th century, in the dining room of a late-18th century London townhouse.*

Far right: *Swagged drapes by Scalamandré, copied from early 19th-century originals in Owens Thomas House, Savannah, Georgia, USA.*

Below right: *Detail of watered silk drapes with tassel fringing. The swags are draped over a gilt metal rosette that has been trimmed with velvet and watered silk.*

Below far right: *Simple swags and tails in a Georgian manor house in Kent, England.*

29

Making swags & tails

Above: *Detail of the tail from the window treatment shown on page 28. The deep multi-coloured fringing defines the shape and folds of the swags and tails.*

MATERIALS

- ◆ Basic sewing kit (see page 146)
- ◆ Main fabric
- ◆ Paper for pattern and pencil
- ◆ Chain or heavy cord
- ◆ Masking/drafting tape
- ◆ Matching or contrasting lining fabric
- ◆ Curtain heading tape
- ◆ 5cm (2in) cotton tape
- ◆ Bullion fringing and flanged rope
- ◆ Tassels
- ◆ Lath or board (2.5cm [1in] thick; 10cm [4in] deep)
- ◆ Brass tacks (or tacks and staples)

Swags and tails create a traditional, quite formal 19th-century look. They are fixed to a lath or board that is slightly wider than the window and the curtain track is fixed to the wall under the lath or board so that the curtains do not interfere with the swags. The main key to success is to calculate the fabric accurately and not to skimp. Good proportions are important in this type of treatment. As a general rule, a pleasant balance is achieved if the length of the swags (at their deepest point) is about a fifth of the measurement from the top of the lath or board down to floor level. The tails should be about half-way down the overall drop. However, in the treatment described here and seen on page 28 a high ceiling allows the swags and tails to be cut much deeper, creating a particularly luxurious look. Also, the inner edges of the tails are slightly angled, so that the folds are narrower at the top than the bottom. As the reverse sides of the tails are visible, they should be lined either with the main fabric or with an attractive matching or contrasting fabric.

1 To calculate the fabric required for the swags mark the finished width of the top of each swag on the lath, using tacks. Attach a length of chain or heavy cord between the two tacks to give the outline of one swag. Make a note of the finished width at the top and the finished depth in the middle. Then remove the chain – the length of the chain equals the bottom width of the swag.

Make a paper pattern as above. Start with a rectangle measuring twice the depth of the finished swag by the bottom width of the swag. Mark out one side and fold it over down the middle and cut out the other side in the same way. Draw a gentle curve at the bottom edge. The top measurement is approximately one-third of the finished width of the swag. Draw diagonal lines to join the top to the bottom – the resulting curved wedge shape is the pattern. Cut out each swag from main lining fabric, adding a 1.5cm (⅝in) seam allowance around the curved edge and 5cm (2in) on all other edges. Swags cut on the bias of the fabric will drape more easily, but this is not always possible with patterns and weaves.

2 Next make a paper pattern for the tails. The width at the top equals the front of the lath including the return, plus twice as much again for each fold. The outer edge equals the maximum length of the tails; the inner edge equals the depth from the top to the point where the angled hemline begins. The sloping bottom line will be the diagonal hem. Cut out each tail from main and lining fabric, adding 5cm (2in) at the top edge and 1.5cm (⅝in) on all other edges.

3 To make up each swag, with right sides facing, pin, baste and machine-stitch the main and lining fabric together along the bottom, curved edge, taking a 1.5cm (⅝in) seam allowance, then turn right side out and press. (For a traditional hand finish, turn in and press the seam allowance of the bottom edge on both fabrics, then, with wrong sides together, slip-stitch the lining to the back of the main fabric along the curved edge.) Baste the lining and main fabric together along the remaining edges. Hand sew the bullion fringe to the bottom edge.

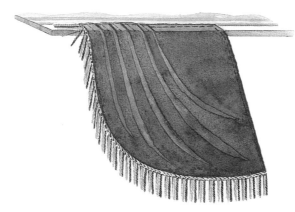

4 Using masking or drafting tape, fix a length of cotton tape – the finished width of a swag, plus 5cm (2in) for turning in the ends – to the edge of a work surface, such as a table or shelf. Mark the middle of the swag on the tape. Working from the bottom curved edge, make four or five rough pleats first one side of the swag, pinning it to the tape, and then the other. The folds at each side overlap the unpleated top edge of the wedge shape. Machine-stitch across the folds and through the tape to hold in place. Turn in the ends of the tape, trim raw edges, then make a second row of machine stitching along the top edge. Attach the swag, with its backing tape, to the pelmet board with tacks or staples.

5 To make up each tail, with right sides together, pin, baste and machine-stitch the main and lining fabric together along the sides and sloping lower edge, taking a 1.5cm (⅝in) seam allowance.

Turn the tail right side out; press the seams. Baste the lining and main fabric together along the top edge. When the tail is pleated the diagonal line will form the zig-zag hem. Starting at the top, hand sew the fringing to the tail along the short inner edge and the bottom diagonal edge.

6 Fix a length of cotton tape, the finished width of a tail plus 5cm (2in) for turning in the ends, to the edge of a suitable work surface. Mark the length of the return on the tape. Starting with the short side edge, form three or four pleats of the same size, leaving enough fabric for the return. Pin the tail to the tape. Machine-stitch through the pleats and tape to hold in place. Turn in the ends of the tape, trim raw edges, then make a second row of machine stitching along the top edge.

7 Tack or staple the pleated section of the tails to the front of the lath and the remaining flat section to the return. Fold the fabric into a mitre to turn the corner. If you are using tassels, arrange them in place in the middle (stagger them slightly so that they hang at different levels, as seen in the photograph on page 28). Stretch the flanged rope all along the top edge of the pelmet and tack or staple it in position to complete the window treatment.

Left, Far left & Below: *A great deal of historical research went into the restoration of the Calhoun Mansion, built in the 1870s in Charleston, Carolina, USA. The swagged, blue damask drapes in the dining room are mainly decorative and reflect the opulence of the house. Note the wooden shutters, which are historically correct for the period.*

Right: *Swagged, silk damask drapes with deep fringing, in a drawing room at the Calhoun Mansion. Like the drapes left and below, they are by Buzz Harper and are based on Empire designs.*

Below centre: *Heavy, silk damask drapes with deep fringing and rosettes, in the dining room at Gloucester, a Neo-classical villa built in 1803 in Natchez, Mississippi, USA.*

Above: *Swagged, silk damask drapes copied from a fashionable 1860s design, in the parlor of Cedar Grove, Vicksburg, Mississippi, USA. The "puddling" of the drapes (where the fabric spills onto the floor) is a statement of status and wealth.*

Left: The furnishings are in the style of the mid-1850s, and the silk damask drapes are copied from original designs.

Left: Silk damask drapes swagged over Empire-style spear-and-star poles in the Ladies' Sitting Room at the High Victorian Calhoun Mansion, USA.

Right & Below: Elaborate silk damask pelmets or cornices and swagged drapes in the Gallery, used as an art gallery, music room and ballroom at the Calhoun Mansion, USA.

Making elaborate swags

MATERIALS
- Basic sewing kit (see page 176)
- Main fabric
- Lining fabric
- Paper and pencil for patterns
- 5cm (2in) cotton tape
- Tassel fringe
- Cord
- Tassels
- Boards, brackets and fixings
- Chain
- Tacks

Lavish and sumptuous, these brocade drapes demand a large room with a high ceiling and other period-style furnishings of the same standard. Meticulous planning, layer by layer, is the key to success in achieving this effect. Time spent in estimating fabric quantities required and making toiles from old sheeting will be well rewarded. To allow the successive layers to hang freely, the curtain track should be fixed to the wall. The main deep swags and tails and the central cone hang from a board, while the upper frieze of small swags hangs from a second board that projects beyond the first. The weight of the finished drapes is considerable, so take great care to make sure that boards and tracks are very securely fixed.

Left: *Swagged and draped treatments gradually became more elaborate toward the end of the 19th century. This is a pastiche of such a treatment.*

1   The main board should extend beyond the track for about 10cm (4in) at the front and sides; the second board (fixed when the main swags are in situ) should extend some 7.5cm (3in) at the front and the sides beyond the first. Alternatively, it is possible to buy special valance creators designed to hold swags, which can be screwed to the wall either side of the curtain track.

2   Secure the board to the wall with screws. Fix the curtain track to the wall underneath the board (if necessary screwing through the back section of the board).

3   To estimate how much fabric you will require for the curtains see pages 149–50, allowing extra length for the fabric to spill onto the floor, even when tied back. The traditional way to make curtains is to cut the lining and main fabric the same size and then to bind the edges together with braid. For these very full drapes it is easier to sew them by machine. You can make the curtains in the same way as for the ruffled-edged drapes on pages 46–7. Substitute the ruffles with the fringing, leaving out the contrast edging and adding fringing to the bottom edge.

4   To make the main swags see pages 30–1. As the swags here are very full, you will need to allow a much greater depth when making the pattern

– up to four times the finished depth, depending on how many folds you desire. Tack the finished swags in place on the main pelmet board. Add decorative ropes, echoing the folds of the swags.

5 Cut out and make the tails in the same way as the tails on pages 30–1, but make both side edges vertical and allow for the extra pleats and length. Hand sew the fringe before attaching the tail to the board.

6 For the central pipe, make a paper pattern. Note the length and width of the finished pipe. Draw a rectangle measuring the length of the finished pipe plus twice the depth of the fringe, by about three times the finished width. Draw a curve along the top edge. The bottom edge is also curved and should measure about one-fifth of the top. Join the top and bottom points with diagonal lines. Cut out one piece of main fabric, adding 5cm (2in) to the top edge and 1.5cm (⅝in) to the sides. Using tailor's chalk and measuring up from the bottom edge, make a curved line a third of the way up. Between this line and the bottom edge run a gathering thread (a). Turn up the seam allowance to the wrong side on the bottom edge and hem. Pin the pleats in place at the top edge and along the chalk line, as shown (b). Machine-stitch to hold the pleats

in place. Pull the gathering thread to make it the same width as the lower pleats. Place the cone right side down, fold over the bottom edge so that the gathers lie on top of the lower pleats, pin and then machine-stitch. Fold back down the bottom edge and you will have formed the frill (c). With right sides facing, machine-stitch the side edges together. Turn the cone right side out. With the seam down the back, baste the top edges together. Hand sew a tassel at the bottom and slipstitch the gap closed. Hand sew fringing at the top of the frill. Attach the cone to the board with tacks.

7 The small swags can be attached to the second board before it is fixed in place. To work out how many small swags you will need to make, pin two contrasting lengths of chain along the board overlapping each other (see pages 30–1). Then start making the underlying, triangular swags. Make a paper pattern. Draw a triangle: the top will be the required width, plus about four equal-sized pleats; the length will be the finished depth – mark this point and then draw the sides. Cut out the swags from main and lining fabric, adding 1.5cm (⅝in) seam allowances to each side and 5cm (2in) to the top.

8 For each triangular swag, with right sides of lining and main fabric facing, taking a 1.5cm (⅝in) seam allowance, machine-stitch the sides together. Turn right side out and press. Baste the

top edges together. Form the pleats as in the illustration (below left); pin and then machine-stitch along the top edge to hold in place. Secure the swags to the board with tacks.

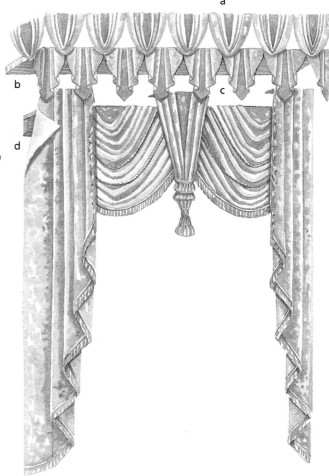

9 Make the top small swags (a) as described on pages 30–1, and fix them to the second board (b) in between the triangular swags (c). Finally, screw the second board to the main board (d).

Lambrequins

Top: *Empire-style silk drapes and lambrequins, copied from Rudolph Ackermann's book* The Repository of Art, *in a 1808 reception room at Nathaniel Russell House, USA.*

Above & Left: *Damask lambrequins with wire edgings, copied from the original window treatment in a bedroom at Lansdowne, a single-storey plantation house built in 1853, in Natchez, Mississippi, USA.*

During the 17th and 18th centuries, the French referred to their flat pelmets or cornices with shaped outlines as *lambrequins* (meaning "scallop"). Fixed above doors or windows, they were usually combined with drapes held with tie-backs. Where pull-up drapes were used, they hid the bunches of fabric formed when these were drawn above the window.

Lambrequins were not used in Britain and America until the 1830s and, unlike the earlier French versions, the term was used to describe a flat pelmet or cornice with shaped outline that extended down the sides of the window or door, and sometimes reached as far as the floor.

Made of stiffened buckram, paper or wood, and usually lined with Holland or plain chintz, lambrequins were covered in a wide range of fabrics, such as velvet, moreen, damask and even cut-up Chinese hangings. Often they were also extensively embellished with trim. Shapes varied enormously, and depended on the style of the particular room.

The heyday of the lambrequin came during the third quarter of the 19th century, particularly in Neo-Renaissance and Victorian-Gothic interiors. However, they had virtually disappeared by the 1890s. The fact that they blocked out a substantial amount of natural light rendered them obsolete as the fashion for brighter interiors dawned in the 20th century.

Right: *The silk damask lambrequins in the library at Gloucester Mansion, in Natchez, Mississippi, USA, were inspired by 19th-century Empire-style designs.*

Making a lambrequin

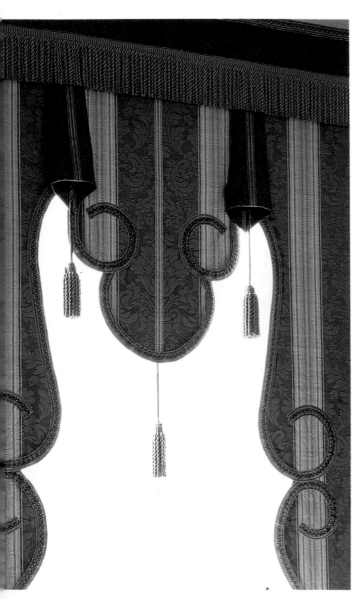

MATERIALS
- ◆ **Basic sewing kit (see page 146)**
- ◆ **Main fabric**
- ◆ **Lining fabric**
- ◆ **Stiff interlining**
- ◆ **Buckram**
- ◆ **Fringe**
- ◆ **Lining paper for pattern and pencil**
- ◆ **Flexible curve, plate or saucer**
- ◆ **Braid**
- ◆ **Fabric adhesive**
- ◆ **Pelmet or cornice board (2cm [¾in] thick)**
- ◆ **Brackets and fixings**
- ◆ **Small brass rings and hooks**
- ◆ **Touch-and-close tape**
- ◆ **Three tassels**

A lambrequin was originally a fabric covering used to keep the sun off a metal helmet. By the early 19th century the word lambrequin was being applied to elaborately scrolled furnishing pelmets or cornices, that were displayed over windows, doors, shelves or mantelpieces. Lambrequins are made by covering a wooden base with fabric or stiffening the fabric with interlining and buckram. The one featured here is fixed behind a fringed pelmet or cornice. It is inter-lined with a translucent material, allowing a certain amount of light to shine through. In the 19th century a woven interlining would have been used, but these days we have the advantage of being able to choose either a non-woven stiff interlining or stiff double-sided self-adhesive sheets of plastic material, produced especially for pelmets or cornices. As with other window treatments, the lambrequin can be fixed outside the window frame to minimize light loss.

1   Start by making the fringed pelmet or cornice. Take the main and lining fabrics and cut out the pelmet to the width (the front of the pelmet board, including the return) and depth, adding 1.5cm (⅝in) seam allowances all around. Cut the same-size piece, minus the seam allowances, from interlining and buckram (see ruffled-edged drapes on page 49).

2   Lockstitch the interlining to the wrong side of the main fabric and then use herringbone stitch to attach the buckram. Press the seam allowances over the interlining and buckram to the wrong side; baste in place. Machine-stitch the braid and fringing in place along the top and lower edges. Remove the basting stitches at the top and bottom.

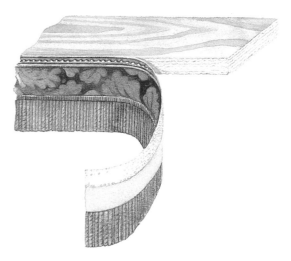

3   Turn in the seam allowances around the lining section and slipstitch it to the back of the main section. On the lining side hand-stitch the hooked side of the touch-and-close tape to the top edge and glue the other side to the front edge of the board.

Above: *An elaborate lambrequin with a fringed pelmet tassels and swirling braid help define the Moorish shape.*

4 To make the lambrequin it is easier to work in sections: one middle and two pieces at each side (unless your window is fairly small and you can cut out the shape from one width of fabric). Make a note of the measurement of each piece, taking the maximum measurements lengthways and widthways and adding 1.5cm (⅝in) seam allowances all around.

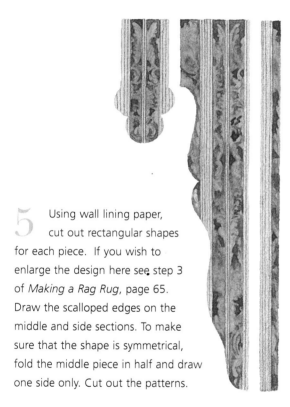

5 Using wall lining paper, cut out rectangular shapes for each piece. If you wish to enlarge the design here see step 3 of *Making a Rag Rug*, page 65. Draw the scalloped edges on the middle and side sections. To make sure that the shape is symmetrical, fold the middle piece in half and draw one side only. Cut out the patterns.

6 Next place the patterns on the main fabric and cut out each section (one side front section will be a mirror image of the other). Cut out the same from lining fabric. Finally, cut each pattern from interlining, without the seam allowances.

7 Take each piece of main fabric in turn and place the corresponding piece of interlining on the wrong side. Using herringbone stitch, and taking stitches through either the interlining only or the seam allowance of the main fabric, attach the interlining to all the straight edges (including the edges where the sections will be seamed together). Along each curved front edge, turn the seam allowance over the interlining to the wrong side. You will need to make slits in the seam allowance and take notches from it (see page 147) to achieve a smooth finish. Topstitch close to the foldline along all curved edges. Repeat this process on all sections.

8 With right sides together and taking 1.5cm (⅝in) seam allowances, join the straight side sections to the curved side sections and then the sides to the middle section. Press the seams flat. Along the top, sides and bottom edges, fold the seam allowance of the main fabric over the interlining and baste in place.

9 Join the lining pieces together into one complete piece and press the seams. Turn in, press and baste all seam allowances. With wrong sides together, slipstitch the lining to the main fabric around the curved shaping and the lower edge. At the top, the sides and the bottom you can either slipstitch, or topstitch by machine through all layers. Remove all basting stitches.

10 Before gluing the braid in position, draw the curlicues on the fabric using tailor's chalk. To make sure that opposite curves are the same, you may find it helpful to use a flexible curve, available from artist's supply stores. This can be shaped into the desired curve and then used like a ruler or a template. Alternatively, use a plate or a saucer to draw the curves. With fabric glue fix the braid around the curved edges and the bottom edge of the lambrequin. For a large amount of gluing, such as this, a glue gun is most useful. Before gluing the braid to the middle section, insert the cord of a tassel underneath the braid.

11 Using the same basic technique described on page 113, make two trumpets, each lined either with main fabric or with lining fabric. Hand-stitch a tassel to the inside of each trumpet. Pin the trumpets in position at the top edge of the lambrequin so that they cover the front side seams and hand stitch.

12 Fix small hooks around the edge of the underside of the pelmet or cornice board. Secure the board to the wall with brackets. Finally, sew small curtain rings to the top edge of the lambrequin and hang the lambrequin from the small hooks under the pelmet or cornice board.

1

2

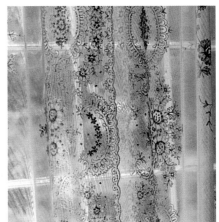

3

4

Sheers

Sheers, or semi-transparent drapes, have been used since the 16th century – mainly to moderate the effects of sunlight entering a room, but also to provide a degree of privacy. Gauze was often pinned over Italian windows in the late 16th century, while in the 17th and early 18th century many European shutterless windows were covered with sashes (thin silks or linens stretched over wooden frames and soaked with oil to make them translucent).

Sashes were still in use in the 18th century, although thin taffeta, half-silks ("siamoise") and muslin, hung from poles, gradually superseded them. First made in India, muslin was mostly white or cream and sometimes woven with a ribbed stripe or small motif.

By the early 19th century, silk or muslin under-curtains, often with tie-backs, had become standard in Regency- and Empire-style interiors. They usually incorporated delicate fringing or border designs in contrasting colours. Generally, they were tied to one side of the window – but were occasionally drawn.

Layered window treatments remained in vogue until the end of the Victorian era. Silk, or Swiss lace on a voile backing, was the preferred choice for under-curtains. However, muslin or machine-made Nottingham lace provided a less expensive alternative. Semi-transparent blinds or shades were also used, sometimes painted with pictures and motifs. By the start of the 20th century a reaction had set in: Edith Wharton dismissed sheers on the grounds that "lingerie effects do not commune well with architecture".

5   **6**

1 *Original lambrequins and late 19th-century Nottingham lace under-curtains at Green Leaves, an 1838 Greek-revival house in Natchez, Mississippi, USA.*

2 *Late 19th-century lace under-curtains.*

3 *French lace curtains, in a medieval townhouse.*

4 *Lace under-curtains such as these were very fashionable in the southern states of the USA from the mid- to late 19th century, and were often imported from Brussels.*

5 & 6 *Embroidered lace under-curtains, also from Green Leaves, were typical of window treatments in American houses prior to the Civil War.*

Left & Above: *Two examples of modern floral chintz in an 18th-century manor house in Norfolk, England. During the 17th and 18th centuries, chintz (or "chintes") was imported from India as dress and furnishing fabric. Made of cotton, and usually glazed or starched, the earlier examples were hand-painted or hand-blocked. During the 19th century, European and American manufacturers began to mass-produce printed chintz to meet an ever-increasing demand. Traditionally, chintz is decorated with floral motifs. However, plain versions are produced, and during the second half of the 19th century some geometrically patterned chintzes were made as well (with the floral motifs being incorporated within a grid of vertical and horizontal lines).*

Chintz

Brightly coloured, hand-painted or hand-blocked calicoes, known as *indiennes* or "chints", first appeared in France at the end of the 16th century. Initially imported from India, they were embellished with animal, bird, fruit and floral motifs (mainly the latter) and used throughout most of Europe during the 17th century for window-, bed- and wall-hangings. Their popularity was in no small part due to their low cost and the fact that the dyes used had been rendered colourfast by the technique of fixing with metal salts (mordants).

Chintzes remained highly sought after in the 18th century but severe restrictions on imports, and on European printers wishing to produce hand-blocked copies, were introduced by governments wishing to protect the wool industry. However, the raising of restrictions in the 1770s soon resulted in a surge in both imports and home production. Colours and patterns were adapted to suit European and American tastes.

During the 19th century, chintzes (now often glazed) depicted subjects as varied as architecture, literary figures and birds. However, the vast majority were floral-patterned. Initially, most French and English chintzes portrayed flowers and plants in stylized form. Thereafter, however, designs in Europe and America became ever more naturalistic – largely due to the introduction of aniline dyes and improvements in mechanized printing. The latter also made chintzes affordable to the growing middle classes.

Left: *Faded floral chintz drapes, by Bennison, in an 18th-century manoir in the Dordogne, France. Chintz tends to fade quite rapidly when exposed to sunlight.*

Bottom left: *Co-ordinating window treatments with other furnishings in the room proved popular for much of the 19th century. The floral chintz used is by Colefax and Fowler.*

Below: *Simply pleated, tie-back chintz drapes, by Bennison, in a medieval manoir, Lot et Garonne, France.*

45

Making ruffled-edged drapes

MATERIALS
- Basic sewing kit (see page 146)
- Main fabric
- Lining fabric
- Plain fabric in a contrast colour, for binding, edging and piping
- Interlining and buckram
- Piping cord
- Curtain heading tape
- Touch-and-close tape
- Pelmet or cornice board (2cm [¾in] thick)
- Brackets and fixing screws

Ruffles can be used with great success on the lower edges of valances and the leading edges of curtains. A valance usually hangs from a separate track in front of the main curtain track. In this treatment the ruffled valance is attached to a fabric pelmet or cornice which in turn is attached to a board. If the board can be set some way above the window frame, the valance will cut out less light, and the windows will look taller. Against tall windows, the arched shape can be more exaggerated than here, with sides up to twice as deep as in the middle. As a general guide to proportions, a valance should be about one-sixth of the length of the curtains in a room with a low ceiling and one-fifth of the length in a room with a high ceiling. The valance can either be attached to the pelmet or cornice board with touch-and-close fastening or by attaching small rings to the pelmet and looping these over nails fixed to the edge of the board (see page 125).

Left: *Here each window has an elaborately ruffled and piped valance, with a graceful arch, which complements curtains with matching ruffled and bound edges.*

1 Make the pelmet or cornice board the length of the curtain track plus 5cm (2in), and 13–15cm (5–6in) wide. If you are fixing the curtain track to the board, place it 5–7.5 cm (2–3in) back from the front edge, to allow free movement. Glue the touch-and-close tape to the edge of the board and fix the board to the wall with brackets (use a central bracket to support the valance if it is over 1.5m (5ft) long.

2 For each curtain, allow twice the measured width (see pages 149–50) for fullness, and add 5.5cm (2⅛in) to the finished length. Allowing for any pattern repeats, cut and join widths together, using flat seams. Make up the lining in the same way.

3 To make the ruffles cut and join strips of fabric. Each finished strip should be twice the finished length of the curtain (more for an even fuller effect) by about 6cm (2½in) wide, plus a 1.5cm (⅝in) seam allowance on all edges. At each short end, turn under and stitch a neat 6mm (¼in) double hem. Run a double gathering thread down one long edge (this will be the edge joined to the curtain) – one row along the 1.5cm (⅝in) seam line and the second row just within the seam allowance.

4 If you are making your own binding for the ruffles cut out long strips of contrasting fabric on the bias (see pages 148–9). For a binding 1cm (⅜in) deep, cut the strips 3cm (1¼in) wide. Make the finished length the same length as the ruffles. Join the strips of fabric together and then press in a narrow 5mm (¼in) hem to the wrong side along both the short and long edges. Bring the long folded edges together and press the binding in half. To bind each ruffle, place the binding strip over the long (ungathered) edge and machine the strip in place, stitching through both folded edges and the ruffle, as above. Alternatively, if you do not want the stitching to show on the right side of the ruffle, use the method shown on page 149.

5 For the edging, between the ruffle and the main curtain, cut and join lengths of contrast fabric to make a long strip 3cm (1¼in) wide by the length of the curtain. With right sides matching and the raw edge of the contrast strip positioned 2.4cm (1in) in from the leading edge of the main fabric (the one that will be ruffled), machine-stitch in place taking a 6mm (¼in) seam allowance. Press the contrast strip over toward the leading edge so that both raw edges meet. Repeat the process for the other curtain(s).

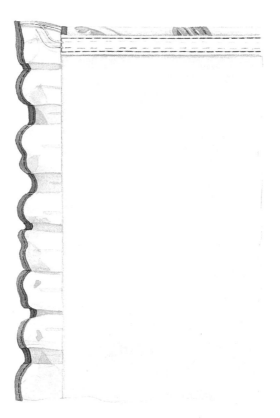

allowance throughout. Turn the curtain right side out. Press the seams so that the ruffle faces outward and at the bottom edge neither the main or lining fabric shows on the other side.

6 For each curtain gather the ruffle to fit the length of the leading edge (the edge with the contrast strip). With right sides facing, raw edges together and taking a 1.5cm (⅝in) seam allowance, pin and then machine-stitch the ruffle to the curtain, starting 4cm (1½in) below the top edge and finishing 1.5cm (⅝in) above the bottom edge.

7 Place the lining on the main fabric right sides together, with the ruffle facing inward, and machine-stitch down both sides and along the lower edge of the curtain, taking a 1.5cm (⅝in) seam

8 At the top, fold over both raw edges of fabric to the wrong (lining) side by 4cm (1½in). Pin the heading tape in position, 2.5cm (1in) below the folded edge, covering the raw edges of fabric. Turn under the edges of the tape at the sides of the curtain and machine-stitch the tape along its top, bottom and side edges (take care to leave the drawing cords free).

9 The valance is made in much the same way as the curtains but it will be slightly wider because of the reveal. Measure the width of the pelmet or cornice board including the reveal and allow twice this measurement by the required depth (valances are usually one-sixth of the finished length of the curtains), plus 1.5cm (⅝in) seam allowances on all edges. Cut out sufficient widths of fabric (main and lining) by the required depth to make up the full width of the valance. Join the widths together. Next make a paper pattern (wall lining paper is useful for the purpose) so as to get an even curve in the middle of the valance, drawing only half of the pattern as above. Place the pattern on the folded fabric and cut out the valance from main and lining fabric.

10 For the ruffle you will need a piece of fabric twice as long as the ungathered valance by the same depth used for the curtain. Cut and join strips of contrast edging as in step 5. Follow steps 3 to 7 to make and attach the ruffle and contrast edging at the lower, curved edge of the valance, and to attach the lining. Turn the valance right side out and press the seams. Along the top edge run two parallel rows of gathering threads on the seamline and just within the seam allowance.

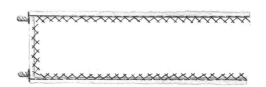

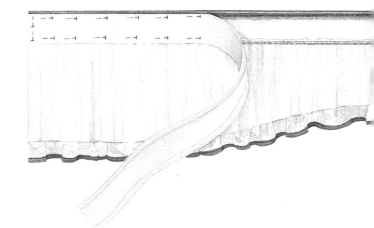

11 The valance is gathered onto a straight pelmet or cornice with piped edges. Cut this out from main and lining fabric to the width of the pelmet board including the reveal, and to the desired finished depth (about a quarter to a third of the finished depth of the valance), adding 1.5cm (⅝in) seam allowances all around. Cut out the same shape from interlining and buckram without seam allowances.

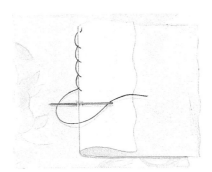

12 Lay the interlining on the wrong side of the main fabric. To lockstitch in place secure the thread to the back of the interlining at the top in the middle; fold the interlining back and, picking up only a couple of threads of each fabric, take a small stitch through the interlining and main fabric, close to the fold; take the needle through the

resulting loop of thread and make another stitch 5cm (2in) further down the fold; fasten off the thread at the bottom edge. Make vertical lines of lockstitches outward at intervals of approximately 20cm (8in).

13 Cut out the bias strips of contrast fabric to cover the piping cord; join the strips together. Cover sufficient piping cord to run along the top and bottom edges of the interlined section (see page 148). With raw edges together, machine-stitch the covered piping cord in position on the right side of the main fabric.

14 Position the buckram on the wrong side of the piped section and herringbone stitch in place (see page 147).

15 Next gather the valance to fit the lower edge of the pelmet or cornice. With right sides together and using the zipper foot to get close to the piping, stitch the valance to the lower edge of the pelmet or cornice. Turn in the seam allowances along the top and sides of the pelmet or cornice, securing the ends of the piping neatly at the back.

16 Turn in the seam allowances on all edges of the lining. Pin the lining to the back of the pelmet or cornice and slipstitch in place.

17 Finally hand sew the hooked side of the touch-and-close tape to the top edge of the valance. Secure the valance in position.

Edgings

During the 15th and 16th centuries hand-sewn decorative edgings and other trimmings were popular in Italy, but were not widely used else-where in Europe (nor were window drapes during this period). However, during the 17th century the fashion for decoratively embellished hangings spread to England and France.

Under the reign of Louis XIV of France, increasingly intricate trimmings (*passementerie*) appeared in royal residences and houses of the nobility. Most had a practical purpose; invariably they were designed to disguise seams in joined lengths of fabric. However, their decorative role also increased, and galloons, braids and fringes of silk and gold and silver thread became the height of fashion.

When the Huguenots emigrated from France to avoid religious persecution at the beginning of the 18th century, they took with them their highly developed *passementerie* skills. The result in England, much of the rest of Europe and then America was a proliferation of exquisite trimmings to augment the increas-ingly elaborate curtain drapery.

Right through to the end of the 19th century, tie-backs were braid-edged and appliquéd. The braids themselves were often embellished with flowers, bows and a variety of Neo-classical, Classical and other revival-style motifs. Silk fringes, became highly popular, and were often combined with ropes, cords and an enormous variety of tassels. The bell-like tufts of the "campaign" fringe proved the most enduringly fashionable.

2

3

4

1 *Silk rope edging, embellished with rows of mini double-tassels, on drapes in a reception room at Nathaniel Russell House, in Charleston, South Carolina, USA.*

2 *Mini double-tassels on the swagged-and-tailed drapes in the dining room of Nathaniel Russell House, USA. Like the tasselled edging referred to above, the design was based on drawings in Rudoph Ackerman's book, Repository of Art, published in the early 19th century.*

3 *Voile under-curtains with edging and tassels, based on early 19th-century designs by Mesangère.*

4 *Alternate-coloured tasselled edging on drapes at The Briars, a house in Natchez, Mississippi, USA.*

1 *Tasselled edging on a swag-and-tail heading, in a Norfolk manor house, England.*

2 *Bauble-like tassels embellish a silk bullion fringe on drapes in a house in Charleston, South Carolina, USA.*

3 *The original swagged silk pelmet in the Games Room at Green Leaves, a Greek-revival house built in 1838 in Natchez, Mississippi, USA, has its original silk and gilded-wire edging.*

4 *Bullion fringing and contrasting lining has been used to give definition to the pleats and folds of this tail.*

5 *Summer drapes of embroidered Swiss-cotton eyelet, with tassel and crotcheted edging, in Nathaniel Russell House, Charleston, South Carolina, USA.*

6 *A pleated and swagged-and-tailed silk pelmet, with a double-tassel edging, also at Nathaniel Russell House, USA.*

7 *Original silk drapes with braided edging in Melrose Mansion, Natchez, USA. (The drapes are identical to those that hung in the White House during the Civil War.)*

1

2

3

5

4

6

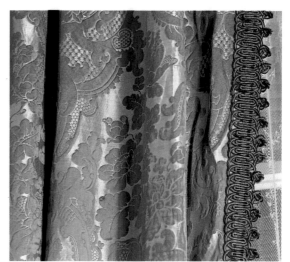

7

Tie-backs & tassels

Apart from their functional role of holding window drapes aside to let in natural light, tie-backs have been appreciated for their decorative contribution to window treatments since the late 16th century. Although sometimes made of plain cord, they have more often been intricate examples of the *passementier's* art, and made to contrast with or match the drapes in question. Prior to the mid-17th century, a contrast was more fashionable.

As well as plaited and ribbon tie-backs, tasselled versions proved very popular from the mid-18th century to the end of the Victorian era. Many types of tassels were available, and made from up to six carved and covered wooden forms. They could be either flat or faceted, and arrow-, screw-, dome- or ball-shaped.

Left: *Silk damask drapes with deep-tasselled and braided silk fringing and tie-backs, at the Calhoun Mansion built in 1860 in Charleston, South Carolina, USA.*

Below: *Multi-coloured, rope-twist silk fringing and damask-covered tie-backs, also at the Calhoun Mansion.*

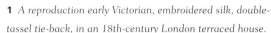

1

2

3

4

5

1 *A reproduction early Victorian, embroidered silk, double-tassel tie-back, in an 18th-century London terraced house.*

2 *Napoleon III-style silk tassels in the Melrose Mansion, Natchez, Mississippi, USA.*

3 *A reproduction of an early Victorian-style, tassel tie-back, from a Georgian house in Kent.*

4 *Drapes and rope-and-tassel tie-backs, copied from the original 19th-century yellow silk-damask drapes at Rosalie, in Natchez, Mississippi, USA.*

5 *Heavy felt drapes, secured with silk-tassel tie-backs in early 19th-century fashion, are in the Empire-style Gentleman's Library at the Calhoun Mansion, USA.*

6 *Original 19th-century silk drapes, edged with a gold wire braid and secured with plain silk rope tie-backs, in a Greek-revival house in Natchez, Mississippi, USA.*

7 & 8 *Modern reproductions of early Victorian cord and tassel tie-backs, such as these, are available from specialist suppliers and some department stores. They are produced in a range of colourways and fibres (such as silk and cotton) and can be co-ordinated with a wide variety of reproduction and original period drapes.*

6

7

8

Making a cord & tassel

MATERIALS
- ◆ Basic sewing kit (see page 146)
- ◆ Thread or yarn in a range of colours
  – fine crochet cottons, wools, linen,
  cottons, flower threads and other
  embroidery threads
- ◆ Cardboard
- ◆ Tapestry needle
- ◆ Strong sewing cotton
- ◆ Braid or wool to wrap around the tassel

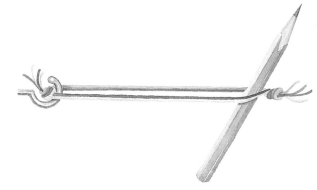

The vogue for cords and tassels as a finishing touch for a wide range of soft furnishings, from swags and tails to armchairs and curtain tie-backs, was at its height in the 19th century, and is enjoying a revival today. Professionally made cords and tassels can be obtained from specialist suppliers, but if you wish to co-ordinate your trimmings to a particular fabric, or would like to experiment with a range of slightly more unusual yarns, tassels and cords are relatively simple to make. A blend of differing yarns and colours can add to the interest, and natural-coloured yarns can be dyed to match your fabric. Use a cold-water dye and form the yarn into loosely tied skeins (if the skeins are tied tightly, the tied areas will not take up the dye). For a range of shades, batch-dye a selection of yarns made from a variety of fibres or fibre blends – different fibres will take up the dye to a greater or lesser extent, giving you a co-ordinating group of yarns to use.

Left: *Here, three multi-coloured, layered and looped woollen tassels with a co-ordinating cord have been made into a curtain tie-back.*

1   If you wish to co-ordinate a cord with a tassel, you can make your own cord, using the same thread or yarn as the tassel. The thickness of the cord depends on the type of thread or yarn and the number of strands used. Experiment with short lengths first, to discover how many you need to use to achieve your desired thickness of cord. For a simple twisted cord, take a strand of each colour used in the tassel; each strand should be three times the length required for the finished cord. Knot the strands together at each end and then fasten one knotted end over a hook (for example, a shelf or door hook). Insert a pencil or knitting needle through the other end, and turn this around so that the strands are twisted together.

2   The strands should be tightly and evenly twisted along their entire length. Once you are satisfied that they are, keeping the cord taut, place your finger in the middle and fold the cord in half, hooking the other knotted end over the hook. When you release the folded end the cord will automatically form into a tight twist, doubling its thickness. Tie the two knotted ends together and smooth the cord with

your hand to even out the twists. For a simple tassel, tie a knot say about 9cm (3½in), depending how long you want the tassel to be, above the folded end of the cord, trim the ends and fringe them out.

3 For a layered and looped tassel like the one pictured left, cut out three pieces of cardboard: one to the required finished depth of the tassel, one slightly shorter, and the third piece even shorter. Wind the thread or yarn around the three pieces of cardboard – the thicker the thread or yarn and the more turns you make, the bulkier the finished tassel will be. If you are using different coloured strands, such as the mixture of blues and neutrals seen here, wind several strands simultaneously around the cardboard. (If you are making several identical tassels, make a note the number of turns you make, to keep each tassel the same thickness.) Next, using a tapestry needle and

strong sewing thread, backstitch along the top edge of each piece of cardboard, making sure that all the strands are linked together in a fringe. (To make a simple, unlayered tassel follow the above instructions but only use one piece of cardboard. And for a slightly different effect, cut through the strands at the lower edge of the cardboard before slipping them off.)

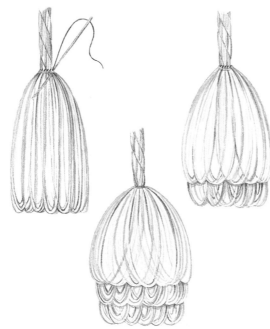

4 Slip the deepest looped fringe off the cardboard, and wrap it around the knotted end of a cord, securing in place by stitching through the backstitched edge and through the knot at the end of the cord. Slip the second fringe off the card and secure in place in the same way around the knotted cord and over the first fringe. Lastly, slip the third, shorter fringe off the cardboard and secure in place.

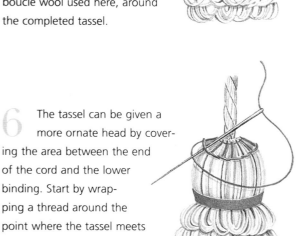

5 When all three looped fringes have been layered in position around the knotted end of the cord, tie off with strong cotton around the threads below the the knot to form the rounded tassel-head shape. Finish by wrapping an attractive contrasting braid or wool, such as the strong blue bouclé wool used here, around the completed tassel.

6 The tassel can be given a more ornate head by covering the area between the end of the cord and the lower binding. Start by wrapping a thread around the point where the tassel meets the cord and secure it. Using this ring of thread as a base, make blanket stitches over the ring and into the tassel below. Continue to work around in rows of blanket stitch until you reach the lower binding; work the last row into the binding threads, then take the thread up into the top of the tassel and down, trimming it level with the lower edge of the tassel. If you are skilled at embroidery you can experiment with a range of laid stitches, and to add to the effect you can incorporate beads or contrast threads into the design.

Floor, wall & door treatments

During the course of the 20th century it has become quite common to think of soft furnishings purely in terms of window drapes and upholstery. However, since the Middle Ages as much, if not more, consideration and ingenuity has been put into the use of fabric on floors, walls and doors. Sumptuous rugs, *portières* and elegant wall-hangings have played a major role in the aesthetics of period interiors and even, on occasions, provided inspiration for the desperate. Scarlett O'Hara's conversion of fringed dining room *portières* into a seductive ballgown is legendary.

Above & Right: *Oriental carpets have been exported to Europe since the 15th century. However, their high cost and rarity encouraged European and English manufacturers to produce copies (originally known as turkey work). These provided a less expensive and fashionable alternative from the 16th century onward.*

Formal rugs & carpets

Until the 17th century, rugs and carpets were rarely found in even the grandest of houses and expensive Oriental rugs were used only to cover tables. However, Persian and Turkish carpets began to be used on floors late in the century, as did elaborate woven Savonnerie carpets from France. Less expensive English copies of Oriental imports, known as turkey work, were an acceptable alternative.

By the mid-18th century, woven Aubusson, Axminster and Wilton carpets became available. The "fitted" or wall-to-wall carpet also emerged: strips of cut-pile Wilton were joined, cut to the shape of a room and finished with a border. "Listed" or "Scotch" carpet, woven from strips of cloth, was the less costly alternative.

During the second half of the 18th century, carpets were embellished with Neo-classical designs and often echoed the configuration of plasterwork on the ceiling. In America, hand-knotted pile carpets were produced in Philadelphia from the 1790s, and made into strips that were joined on site.

During the early 19th century, the Brussels weave was introduced; this had a looped rather than a cut pile. Favoured patterns of the period included Egyptian and Classical motifs.

During the Victorian age, large-patterned woven carpets were popular, fitted or unfitted. Oriental carpets, and European copies of these, remained fashionable, while machine-weaving increased both output and affordability.

Left: *Persian carpets featured in many Victorian parlours, particularly during the second half of the 19th century.*

Right: *An original Savonnerie carpet in the early 19th-century Grand Salon, Château de Compiègne, France.*

Below: *A Persian rug on 19th-century parquet flooring.*

Above: *An original 18th-century Aubusson carpet, in the drawing room of a Jacobean manor house in North Wales.*

Above: *A Persian carpet in the drawing room of an American Regency townhouse, restored c.1886.*

Left: *The replica carpet in the music room of a restored American Empire-style house was woven in England and matched to an original American carpet of c.1804–15.*

Right: *A modern reproduction of a stair runner and hall carpet design popular in the late 18th and 19th centuries.*

Far right: *Wall-to-wall carpets, woven to fit the perimeter of a specific room, were expensive, and therefore a statement of wealth by a Victorian home-owner.*

Below far right: *The geometric and floral design of this modern tapisserie carpet is from an 18th-century original.*

Below middle: *A modern carpet, custom-woven and copied from an American Federal design of 1810–30.*

Below: *The period-style carpet has been cut to fit around the central wall division between interconnecting drawing rooms in a Regency house. Red floral bouquets are set against a background of yellow-brown foliage.*

Country rugs

Rush matting was the most commonly used floor-covering in country houses until the middle of the 17th century. From the 18th century onward, in grander country houses, imported Oriental, Middle Eastern and, later, European carpets were frequently placed over rush (and sisal) matting – or even replaced it altogether. During the 18th and 19th centuries, oiled floorcloths made from coarse canvas and featuring stencil-painted patterns provided an alternative to rush, sisal and carpet.

All of these floor-coverings were used in both town and country – but the home-made, rustic rugs which became popular from the late 18th century through to the late 19th century were confined to smaller country homes.

Yarn-sewn pictorial rugs were mainly produced in North America between 1800 and 1840, and were introduced by Pennsylvanian Dutch and German settlers. Usually made with two-ply yarn on a base of home-spun linen or burlap, they incorporated patriotic motifs and original designs of people, ships, houses and animals – as opposed to the traditional English designs of floral and geometric motifs.

Home-made rag rugs, worked from plaited strips of re-used materials, were also common

to country dwellings throughout Europe and America (notably on the bare floorboards of Colonial and Shaker homes). Shirred rugs, in which rags were couched onto the burlap surface, were popular between 1825 and 1860. However, they became less fashionable with the advent of hooked rugs during the late 1840s.

"Drawn-in", or hooked, rugs were made from wool and cotton thread on a foundation of either linen, tow, homespun hemp or, later, Indian jute burlap or hessian. Indigenous to North America, much of their popularity can be attributed to Edward Sands Frost, a Maine tin-peddler who cut designs into metal stencils and stamped the patterns onto burlap grounds. He sold these between 1864 and 1876 directly to housewives, who worked them in wools.

Frost's most popular designs included animals within rope, leaf, floral or geometric borders, although he also used Oriental and Masonic patterns. Patchwork designs in imitation of quilts were also produced, as were motifs copied from Navajo rugs. However, people, ships and landscapes were less common as they required more skill to reproduce.

Left: *A Victorian rag rug and a modern ethnic-style rug laid over sisal matting, in a 19th-century style French bathroom.*

Right: *This "patchwork" hooked rug on an American farmhouse floor complements the "Rolling Star" design quilt displayed on the wall.*

Right: *Native American (Navajo) rugs used as floor and table coverings in a house in Sante Fé, New Mexico, USA.*

Above left: *A brightly coloured, 19th-century rag rug in a medieval manoir in the Lot et Garonne, France.*

Above right: *Queen Victoria's fondness for Scotland was reflected in the popularity of tartan rugs in Victorian homes.*

Making a rag rug

MATERIALS

- ◆ Basic sewing kit (see page 146)
- ◆ Collection of washed fabrics
- ◆ Paper and pen or pencil
- ◆ Fabric marker pen
- ◆ Hessian, the size of the finished rug, plus a 3.5cm (1½in) hem allowance all around
- ◆ Strong button thread
- ◆ Stretcher frame
- ◆ Webbing
- ◆ Rug hook

Traditionally rag rugs were a utilitarian means of recylcing old clothing, furnishings and dressmaking scraps to provide an inexpensive covering for cold floors. The technique used for the rug show here is looping. The loops can be as short or as long as you like; but the more closely worked the rug is the more durable it will be. Loops can also be cut to make a tufted finish. Almost any fabrics can be used for rug-making, including synthetics, though these tend to attract dirt more than fabrics made from natural fibres. Also you should avoid fabrics which fray easily. For a wall hanging it is possible to mix fabric types and to include lightweight fabrics such as silks or sheers, but for a traditional floor rug it is best to use firm cottons or woollens. A large version can take some time (and a lot of fabric) to complete, so it would be best to start with a relatively small bedside rug. You can back your finished work with hessian if you wish, but this can ruck and/or act as a dirt trap.

Left: *Rag rugs are a thrifty way of bringing warmth and colour to the home and the many shades of blue and red used here give this rug a lively texture.*

1 Cut out fabric strips on the cross or bias, making them 5cm (⅝in) wide and as long as possible. Keep strips in bundles of one colour or near-shades and tones, to make working easier.

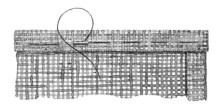

2 Turn under a 3.5cm (1½in) hem on all sides of the hessian (there is no need to mitre the corners) and secure with strong thread, using short basting stitches.

3 Plot your design on the right side of the hessian, using a permanent fabric marker or coloured pencil (do not use an ordinary marker as it will stain the fabrics if the finished rug gets wet). If you wish to use the design shown here, scale it up by copying it onto paper and dividing it into ruled squares. Then on paper the size of the finished design rule off the same number of squares. In each square of the large paper, draw the section of the pattern that is in the corresponding square of the original. Then lay the hessian over the paper and transfer the lines using your permanent marker. If you have difficulty seeing the lines through the hessian, tape both paper and hessian to a window.

4 Hooked rugs are best worked with the hessian base stretched in a wooden frame. If your frame does not have webbing attached, tack webbing to the longest sides of the frame. Using strong thread, stitch the long sides of the hessian to the webbing along the top and bottom of the frame. Lace the sides of the hessian to the sides of the frame, taking the thread either through the holes provided in the frame or around the wood and then through the hessian. The hessian must be evenly stretched and taut or it will be difficult to work and may pull out of shape.

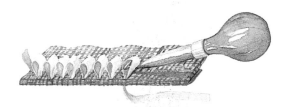

5 Start with the border: holding the end of a strip of fabric at the back of the work, insert the rug hook and bring up a loop of fabric, 12mm (½in) deep, to the front of the work. Continue around the border in this way, bringing up loops at intervals of about 3–6mm (⅛–¼in), until the border is complete. Leave the ends of the strips on the right side.

6 Next, work the main outlines of the design. Then fill in all of the outlined areas until the rug is complete.

7 Finally, remove the stitching attaching the edges of the rug to the webbing and unpick the lacing at the sides.

Alternative method

This type of rug can be made by prodding the loops through from the back of the rug. In this case, mark the pattern on the back of the hessian and work with the wrong side uppermost, pushing loops through to the front with a blunt prodder, such as a chopstick or a blunted screwdriver.

Wall treatments

Tapestries provided an ideal decoration for walls from the Middle Ages to the end of the 16th century. Robust and portable, they were used by the seigneurial classes as they moved from castle to castle. Colourful and exquisitely figured silk velvets, hung from hooks, rings or rods, were also much in evidence, while poorer houses made do with painted cloth hangings.

By the 17th century, as households became less mobile, portable wall-hangings were no longer a necessity. However, tapestries remained fashionable, although they were often cut to fit specific rooms. Turkish and Persian rugs and European turkey work, were also used, as was crewelwork. Gilt leather, silk damask, brocatelle and worsted materials, such as moquette, proved popular. The smartest rooms had heavier hangings for winter and lighter ones for summer. By the mid-17th century, painted cloth hangings were replaced in less affluent homes by patterned dornix.

At this time, hangings were usually supplied in narrow strips, their vertical seams disguised with applied trimmings made of silk or metal threads. Alternating widths of different materials were sometimes used, and there was usually a border around the main field. A panelled effect ("impaning") often created in the field used strips of contrasting material. From the 17th century onward most hangings were stretched and nailed to a framework of

Left: *Monogrammed silk, secured by rings attached to wall-hooks in a "medieval" bedroom, Leeds Castle, Kent, England.*

wooden battens attached to the wall. The nails were masked either by fabric or a fillet of carved and gilded or painted wood.

In the 18th century, the majority of fabrics already mentioned continued to be used for wall-hangings, although patterns changed and new materials were introduced. Tapestries with two-dimensional designs or a limited sense of depth (*verdure*) remained popular, while gilt leather fell out of favour. Among the new materials introduced were Chinese painted silk taffetas (*Pékins*), watered or moiré mohair, worsteds with a striped or moiré effect, satins and Indian painted cottons (*toiles peintes*). Popular types of trimmings included furbelows, ruffles and cappings (*campanes*). The choice of materials for fillets for impaning and hiding seams and nails grew, with papier mâché or composition types that resembled lace or carved moulding becoming available. Thin strips of gilt leather were used for bordering.

The fashionable wall-hangings of the late 18th century remained popular during the first half of the 19th century. Tented walls and ceilings were a feature of grander houses in Empire France, Regency England and Federal America, while hangings in a wide range of historically revived styles appeared in many homes until the 1860s. However, during the latter part of the century an increasing concern that fabrics were dust traps and retained the odours of food resulted in a marked decline in the use of wall-hangings. The development was accelerated by widespread use of mass-produced wallpapers.

Above: *A 17th-century crewelwork wall-hanging adds colour and texture to the wall of a medieval priory in Dorset, England.*

Right: *An 18th-century crewelwork wall-hanging on the wall of a 16th-century manoir in France.*

Below & Below right: *A 1930s reproduction of Genoese silk wall-coverings, in a sitting-room at Leeds Castle, Kent, England. The detail shows the hand-woven silk border featuring one of the tassels.*

67

Left: *An elaborate cotton fabric in a mid-19th century pattern covers the walls of a bedroom in a château of the same period, near Bordeaux, France.*

Right: *Modern cotton Provençale fabrics, by Souleiado, are pleated on the bedroom walls of a 19th-century château.*

Far right: *A late 18th-century tôile de Jouy on the walls of a bedroom in a 19th-century Dordogne château, France.*

Below: *A modern reproduction tôile, mounted on wooden battens, lines the walls of a bedroom, London, England.*

Below right: *An 18th-century French bibliotèque with its original Beautiran fabric backing.*

How to cover walls in fabric

Above: *Detail of the fabric-covered wall (opposite), featuring the casing for the curtain wire and the small frill at the top.*

MATERIALS

- ◆ **Basic sewing kit (see page 146)**
- ◆ **Fabric**
- ◆ **Curtain wire, screw eyes and hooks**
- ◆ **Wooden battens, fixings and screws**

Walls were originally covered in fabric as this provided a good form of insulation and was useful in hiding poor surfaces. While fabric can still be used for practical reasons, today it is more often used decoratively. Fabric-covered walls can complement a lavish period-style window treatment, carrying the theme around the room. Although the effect may be sumptuous, it is relatively easy to achieve if, as here, the fabric is simply gathered onto curtain wires attached to the wall. There may be suitable fixing points for the hooks to carry the wires, such as picture rails, skirting/ base boards or dado rails, but if not, battens can be screwed to the wall behind the top and bottom edges of the fabric. For the treatment featured here choose a lightweight or sheer fabric, such as lawn, organdie or, for true luxury, silk. Modern silk-effect fabrics may not be authentic to the period you are aiming for, but they can look good and have many advantages, including washablility and economy. If you wish to use patterned fabric, allow for any pattern repeats.

1 Fix hooks, or battens and hooks, in position to carry the curtain wires. If necessary, fix extra battens above and below doors, windows and electrical outlets (turn off the mains electricity when fixing battens around outlets). If you intend to hang pictures, choose where they will go and fix battens to the wall at those points.

2 To calculate the amount of fabric needed, measure the length and width of each wall separately. Add 15cm (6in) to the length for the top and bottom casings. For the width you will need enough fabric to make up one-and-a-half times to twice the finished dimension. Cut out the fabric, allowing for any pattern repeats (see pages 149–50).

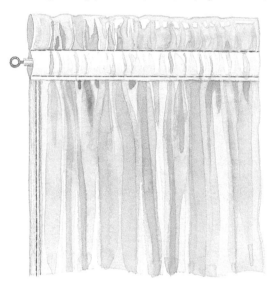

3 Using flat seams and with right sides facing join the fabric widths together; press the seams flat. Press over a double 1cm (⅜in) hem to the wrong side down each side edge and then machine-stitch. To make the casings turn over a double 4cm (1½in) hem to the wrong side along both the top and bottom edges, pin or baste. Machine-stitch close to the folded edges, then make another row of machine stitching 2cm (¾in) above the first at the top, and below the first at the bottom. Thread curtain wires through the casings at the top and bottom and fix the wires in place, adjusting the gathers evenly across the wall.

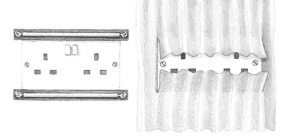

4 If you have to negotiate an electrical socket or switch, mark its position on the fabric with tailor's chalk. Cut the fabric down the sides and across the middle (in an H-shape) of the outlet. Take the curtain down from the wall. Turn the top and bottom edges of the H-shape under to make casings for the short wires. Neaten the sides with binding cut from the same fabric (see page 149).

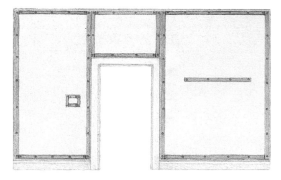

Alternative method

To cover walls with flat rather than gathered fabric, join the fabric widths as in step 3, then staple or tack the fabric to battens. Cover the staples or tacks and all fabric edges with braid or a woven ribbon trim, glued in place with fabric adhesive. This treatment is particularly suitable if you have a strong pattern or a heavier fabric.

Door curtains

The functional purpose of *portières* is to sound- and draught-proof doorways. Since the Middle Ages they have tended to be made of heavier-weight fabrics such as tapestry, velvet, brocatelle and damask. They have also had an important aesthetic role. In 16th-century Europe, pairs of *portières* were often held aside with ropes and tassels and topped by pelmets decorated with appliquéd embroidery. Toward the end of the 17th century, they were increasingly integrated with other fabrics: Daniel Marot's designs show portières en-suite with wall-hangings (linked with a continuous pelmet or cornice). During the 18th century, they often echoed the style and fabric of bed-hangings.

Portières were little used in Britain from the end of the 18th century until the 1850s. They became popular again as many designers used them in the second half of the century, notably Charles Eastlake in the United States. While some decorators felt they should not "repeat the curtains of the room, but represent a separate idea", others advocated double-sided *portières*, so that each would harmonize with the room it faced. Favoured materials included plush, damask, brocatelle, velvet, chenille, and even Turkish rugs. Appliqué and embroidery were often added to divide them into horizontal bands relating to the frieze, field and dado of adjacent walls.

At the beginning of the 20th century, *portières* remained popular in many interiors, particularly where small rooms made doors an inconvenience. After being out of fashion during the First World War, they enjoyed a resurgence during the 1920s and 1930s, and reappeared in a wide variety of lighter fabrics – including mercerized cottons, velours, reps, taffeta, chintz, dimity, cretonnes and jute.

Left: *Fringed tapestry* portières *in an arched doorway at 16th-century Parham House, in Sussex, England.*

Above: *The glazed door in a mid-19th-century château is backed with original cotton Carreaux du Perigord. This example inspired a new range of fabrics by Souleiado.*

Left: *The original, velvet pole-hung* portières *divide the front and back parlours of Green Leaves, a Greek-revival house built in 1838, in Natchez, Mississippi, USA. The front parlour is furnished with its original, mid 19th-century Rococo-revival suite of furniture.*

Far left: *Braided and tasselled tie-backs secure a pair of linen* portières, *trimmed with machine-made tapestry and topped by a fringed pelmet. The room is a late 19th-century interior at Linley Sambourne House, London, England.*

73

Upholstery

The historian Livy scorned the Roman use of coloured stuffs and pillows to pad chairs, considering it "foreign luxury". However, these Roman cushions were but an early instance of an almost universal desire to make furniture both comfortable and aesthetically pleasing. The fashions for covering early 17th-century chairs with tapestry, decorating 18th-century rooms en-suite with matching silk-damask upholstery, curtains and hangings, and springing and deep-buttoning velvet-upholstered seating during the Victorian era are more recent examples. The fabrics that have been preferred for upholstery, notably silk, wool, ather and cottons, have remained perennial favourites – as have the patterns incorporating floral, human and animal motifs or, alternatively, geometrics, such as stripes, checks and dots.

Above & Right: *Looking into the parlour of Monmouth House built in 1818 in Natchez, Mississippi, USA. Recently restored, the room includes a mid-19th century "conversation settee" (seen through the doorway) and a carved, mahogany open armchair. Both are upholstered in a pale-blue silk damask, also used for the drapes.*

Left: *A 17th-century tapestry-upholstered child's chair stands in front of a marble bust on an Empire pedestal in the Gentleman's Library at Monmouth House, Natchez, Mississippi, USA.*

Below: *An early 19th-century English oak copy of a 17th-century turned chair. The stuffed-over seat and the back panel are upholstered in "flame-stitch" needlepoint.*

Tapestry

Tapestry-covered upholstered chairs first appeared in the 1620s (notably on English "farthingales", which were exported to Europe). Leading tapestry centres of the 17th and 18th centuries included: Flanders (in the Low Countries), Mortlake and Worcester (in England), and Gobelins, Beauvais and Aubusson (in France). Popular designs for chair seats and backs included scenes from Aesop's fables, chinoiseries and florals.

Tapestry upholstery declined during the Neo-classical and Classical revivals of the late 18th and early 19th centuries. However, the Gothic Revival and the work of William Morris during the Victorian era restimulated interest. Between 1860 and 1890, numerous chairs in Europe and America featured seat and back covers with applied bands of tapestry. Medieval figures on floral grounds and machine-made "Beauvais" tapestries with scrolls and acanthus leaves were much in favour.

From the 1890s to the 1920s, Baronial style and the Jacobean-revival saw a fashion for machine-made *verdure* tapestries (in slightly faded cottons) for use on chairs, armchairs and sofas, in all manner of traditional patterns.

Above right: *A 17th-century oak chair with its original (restored) upholstery, in Parham House, Sussex, England.*

Right & Far right: *A late 18th-century, upholstered, gilt open armchair, in a Norfolk manor house, England. The close-up of the armchair reveals its exquisitely worked and original seat covered in petit-point.*

77

Left: *A 19th-century, painted French canapé. The tapestry upholstery, depicting red and green flowers and foliage, is original and particularly well-preserved.*

Below: *A Louis XV painted and gilt armchair. The seat, back panel and tops of the arms are covered in silk tapestry featuring elaborate and exquisitely detailed floral motifs.*

Above: Hand-painted, tapestry-style covers on a Louis XV gilded armchair and footstool.

Above left: An 18th-century, painted and upholstered French salon armchair retains its original tapestry cover.

Left: A pair of 19th-century mahogany armchairs, in a manoir on the Dordogne, France. The combination of tapestry covers on the fronts of the chairs and red velvet on the backs was not uncommon – it being considered acceptable to use a less expensive fabric on areas that were rarely seen.

79

Damask & silk

Prior to the invention of the Jacquard loom and mechanized mass-production techniques in the 19th century, figured silk upholstery was the preserve of the wealthy, for reasons of cost.

In grander households of the 15th and 16th centuries, large floor cushions or pillows were covered in silk damask. By the late 17th century, silk damask was being used on upholstered chairs and settees, and remained fashionable in the Palladian, Rococo and Neo-classical interiors of the 18th century. In Empire-style rooms of the 19th century, it was often applied *en-suite* with other furnishings.

Slightly less expensive alternatives to silk damask were also available from the beginning of the 17th century. Linen damask proved the most popular, although woollen and worsted varieties were used (particularly in America). Less expensive stamped, rather than woven, versions, including block-printed cottons, were also available from the late 18th century.

Throughout this period, the traditional damask flat patterns featured stylized flowers and leaves, as well as Near- and Far-Eastern motifs, such as pomegranates. These proved the most popular, while classic colours ranged from crimson, magenta, deep green and royal blue to various pastel shades.

Left: *A mid-19th-century French armchair, upholstered with a silk top cover in a contemporary "wreath" design.*

Right: *A pair of 19th-century gilt chairs, covered in a modern silk fabric inspired by designs from the period.*

Above: *A period-style silk damask on 19th-century French gilt chairs, in an American Neo-classical villa in Mississippi.*

Right: *A mahogany sofa, c.1815 and made in New York, with brass mounts and yellow silk covering, in the Nathaniel Russell House, Charleston, South Carolina, USA.*

Left: *A mahogany dining chair (c.1825–30) upholstered in Scalamandré documentary silksey-woolsey rosette fabric.*

Far left: *An American Regency mahogany chair in red and gold silk, Owens Thomas House, Savannah, Georgia, USA.*

Below left: *An early 19th-century chair with a Regency-stripe silk-covered seat pad, in Nathaniel Russell House.*

Below: *A Regency sofa, covered in green silk with a rosette pattern, in the Melrose Mansion, Natchez, Mississippi,*

Making squabs for a day bed

Above: *The fabric used on this Napoleonic day bed (c.1890) is a striped Watts and Co. design made from silk and cotton.*

MATERIALS

- ◆ **Basic sewing kit (see page 146)**
- ◆ **Cover fabric**
- ◆ **Saucer (to use as a guide)**
- ◆ **Decorative cord trim**
- ◆ **Existing or purpose-made squab and bolsters**
- ◆ **Ticking, if making new casings (this must be feather-proof if you are using a feather or down filling)**
- ◆ **Paper (to make pattern for bolster casing ends)**

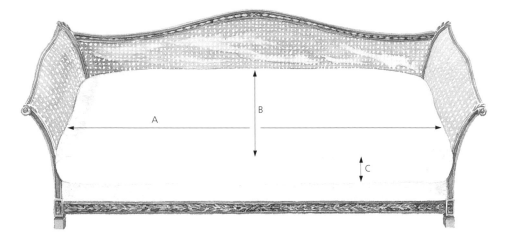

Whatever the style of your day bed, the squabs should be well-filled and luxuriously soft. This can present problems, as the original squabs may have suffered over the years, or have been replaced by less satisfactory ones. It is unlikely that you will find ready-made squabs of the correct size and shape, so you will have to decide whether to repair and refill the existing squabs, make new casings, or have new squabs made. The 19th-century filling would have been down or feathers, and nothing else gives quite the same opulent feeling. Hollow-fill polyester tends to become lumpy with handling. It is wiser to either have feather-filled squabs made to order, or make the casings yourself and have them filled with feathers.

1 Start by estimating how much fabric you will need. For the squab, measure the length A, width B and depth C, adding 1.5cm (⅝in) seam allowances all around to all measurements. Decide whether you need one or more widths of fabric to cover the length of the squab. When joining widths never have a join at the middle. Use one width in the middle and half a width or less placed to each selvedge side of this central panel. Allow for pattern repeats (see pages 149–50). Making sure that the grain is straight and the pattern square, cut out two pieces measuring A x B, plus seam allowances, from cover fabric and also from ticking for new casings. To round off the front corners, use a saucer as a guide and mark the rounded edge on the fabric. Cut out the welt – the total length will be A x 2 plus B x 2 plus extra seam allowances for joins, and the width will be C.

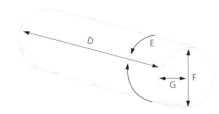

2 For the bolsters measure the length D by the circumference E, and for the gathered end pieces measure the circumference E by the radius G.

Cut out a piece of cover fabric and ticking measuring the length D by the circumference E plus seam allowances, for each bolster. For the gathered ends cut out four oblong end pieces measuring the circumference E by the radius G. Draw a circle on paper to the chosen diameter F. Cut out four end circles from ticking for the casings.

3   To make up each bolster cover, with right sides facing and long edges together pin, baste and machine-stitch each main piece into a cylinder, leaving a gap at the middle of the seam, to insert the pad. Press seams open.

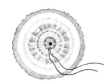

4   With right sides facing and long edges together, pin, baste and machine-stitch end pieces into small cylinders. Run a strong thread 12mm (½in) in from the edge around one end. Pull the thread to form a gathered fabric circle; tie thread tightly, adding a few stitches at the back to secure. With right sides facing, pin, baste and machine-stitch two end pieces to each main cylinder. For a smooth fit make cuts or notches in the seam allowances. Turn right side out.

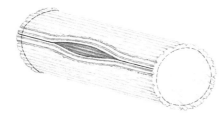

5   Make two new casings for the bolsters as in step 3, leaving a gap at the middle of the seam for filling. Pin, baste and machine-stitch the circular end pieces to the cylinder ends. Make cuts or notches in the seam allowances for a smooth fit. Turn right side out. Once the casing is filled, slipstitch the gap closed. Insert the finished or existing pad into the bolster cover and slipstitch the side seam opening closed.

6   Now start to assemble the squab's top cover. With right sides facing, pin and machine-stitch the welt pieces together to make one length. Press the seams open.

7   With right sides together, pin, baste and machine-stitch the welt to the bottom section, easing the welt around the corners at the front. The seams should fall at the back or sides of the squab,

where they will not be seen. Make cuts or notches in the seam allowances around corners, to ensure a smooth fit. Attach the top section in the same way, leaving a gap down one side edge, for the pad. Turn the finished cover right side out through the gap in the side seam.

8   If you are making a new casing from ticking make in the same way as for the top cover of the squab. To avoid bulk, ensure that the seams for the casing and top cover do not fall in the same place. When the casing has been filled, close the gap in the side seam with slipstitches. Insert the newly filled or existing pad into the top cover, then slipstitch the open side seam closed.

9   Finally, add the cord around the top and bottom seams of the squab and the seams at the ends of the bolsters. Place the joins in the cord unobtrusively at the back or the sides of the squab. Secure matching thread in the seam; place the cord in position and sew through the fabric and into the cord, taking tiny stitches and slipping the needle through the fabric. To join the cord unravel each end a short way, intertwine the strands and secure by neatly stitching together.

Left: *A pair of 18th-century French gilt armchairs, covered in modern, geometrically patterned silk, Charleston, South Carolina, USA.*

Above & Middle *A suite of 19th-century French furniture, upholstered in ivory silk damask.*

Above right: *An Empire chair in ivory silk damask, in the Calhoun Mansion, Charleston, South Carolina, USA.*

Right & Far right: *Ivory silk damask on a 19th-century French gilt armchair, in an 18th-century Charleston house.*

Below: *A modern sofa is given a period feel by heavy silk damask upholstery in a Classical style.*

87

Checks & stripes

Woven or printed checks have been used for upholstery since the early 18th century. The Swedes employed checked cotton or linen chair seats to complement much of their Gustavian furniture. In England, a variety of furniture checks were made from 1750, notably bold-patterned linen weaves from Manchester. Many of these were exported to America and by 1768 furniture checks in Saxon blue, green, yellow, scarlet and crimson were on sale in New York. From 1810, woven checks were also made in Rhode Island, mainly in the blues and browns favoured by German immigrants.

In the early 19th century, checked and plaid gingham was imported from India to Europe (and America) and often used to make slip-covers for chairs. From the 1850s, hard-wearing woollen plaid (or tartan) became popular, and the introduction of aniline dyes encouraged riotously coloured designs. The traditional colours of red, azure, dark blue, bottle green, black and white were most favoured for furniture.

Striped upholstery fabrics were used in Holland at the beginning of the 18th century, but their heyday was from 1750s to the 1820s, notably in Regency England and Napoleonic France. Among the most popular fabrics were coarse-woven silk bourettes and striped gingham. Later, stripes were employed to produce paning effects in Gothic-revival and Neo-Rococo interiors, and they were even incorporated (in grid form) as secondary patterns in traditional floral chintzes.

Opposite: *A 19th-century wirework bench with seat pad and bolster covered in traditional cotton checks and stripes.*

Right: *Louis XIV chairs covered in a traditional Carreaux du Perigord cotton, in a 17th-century French château.*

Below right: *A Trog sofa in traditional yellow-cotton check and a Gustavian armchair in a green cotton. Both are shown in a 1770s house in Odenslunda, Sweden.*

Below: *A Chippendale-style sofa in checked, Delft-colour cotton, in a 1730s Amish log house, USA.*

Velvets & leather

Since the 1620s, velvet has remained a fashion-able and luxurious option for upholstery. In the 17th and 18th centuries, both cut and uncut Genoese silk velvets (often incorporating motifs) were used to upholster chairs either individually or *en-suite* with other furnishings. Woollen velvets were also popular, as were patterned *gaufrage* velvets. During the 19th century, velvet became even more popular (and slightly less expensive), and remained so into the 1920s. This was particularly the case in the United States, where wool velvet ("plush") was most chiefly associated with Aesthetic, Eastlake and Arts and Crafts furniture.

Even more durable than velvet, leather was also widely used from the beginning of the 17th century – initially on "farthingale" chairs, and particularly in dining rooms. Until the mid-18th century, gilt leather proved a fashionable alternative to plain-coloured versions. In addi-tion, the Italian practice of covering chairs in "damask" leather (stamped with motifs from a hot, iron plate) enjoyed a revival in the 1830s. While leather was superseded by many mass-produced fabrics during the 19th century, it did appear again on items of late 19th-century Arts and Crafts furniture (notably those designed by Gustav Stickley).

Left: *A late 19th-century leather armchair and stool, in the hallway of a mid-19th-century château on the Dordogne.*

Below: *A 19th-century, silk-velvet-upholstered, painted and gilt French armchair.*

Above: *The woodwork in the entrance hall of a 17th-century château on the Dordogne, France, has been painted the traditional vert de gris. This is a good backdrop for a 1920s chair with its original fabric and a 19th-century chaise-longue upholstered in a hardwearing red denim.*

Right: *In a stairway hall of a manor house near Bordeaux, France, the 19th-century French open armchair and stool retain their original cut-velvet upholstery.*

Left: *A 19th-century French painted chair upholstered in cut velvet and surrounded by heavy, silk-damask drapes.*

Upholstery styles

Many of the changes in the appearance of furniture have resulted from technical advances in the art of upholstery, notably the development of springs and deep-buttoning (see pages 98–9). However, as with drapes, there has always been a close connection between upholstery styles and changing fashions in dress.

More specifically, chairs and other forms of seating have, like men and women, always been either dressed for an occasion or for comfort – and preferably both. The use of velvet to upholster the seats, arms and stretchers of grander chairs during the 17th century is an example of the latter. Velvet is both a luxurious and practical fabric – aesthetically pleasing, comfortable and providing the degree of friction necessary to avoid slippage on seating.

The 17th- and 18th-century practice of supplying seating with fine-quality, fixed upholstery, together with additional lighter and less expensive slipcovers, is a further example. Hand-woven fabrics, such as silk damask, were permanantly fitted and used on formal occasions and during the winter months. Cotton slipcovers, loosely cut like a housedress, were used during the summer or when formality was not required.

Similarly, as fashions changed during the 17th century, understated pie-crust ruffles were replaced by flamboyant ruching and swagging. In the 19th century, the masculine simplicity of Classical-revival styles was superseded by overtly feminine Neo-Rococo curves and, in turn, by the plumper, bustled look favoured by women during the "High-Victorian" period.

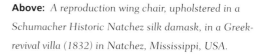

Above: *A reproduction wing chair, upholstered in a Schumacher Historic Natchez silk damask, in a Greek-revival villa (1832) in Natchez, Mississippi, USA.*

Left: *An 18th-century French armchair upholstered in a traditional-style floral patterned silk damask – flowers being one of the most common motifs of the period.*

Far left: *An unusual French faux leopardskin silk velvet, on a gilt 19th-century French chair in a modernized late 18th-century townhouse in Charleston, South Carolina, USA.*

Right: *It has become fashionable to use artificially aged chintz to give a period feel to reproduction chairs (as here). The contrasting needlepoint cushion or pillow is in keeping with this style of upholstery.*

Making loose covers

Above: *The striped damask fabric used on this traditional armchair gives the chair a rather formal appearance.*

MATERIALS

- ◆ Basic sewing kit (see page 146)
- ◆ Upholstery fabric
- ◆ Graph paper for pattern and pencil
- ◆ Four braid rosettes or covered buttons
- ◆ Upholstery nails
- ◆ Piping cord
- ◆ Press fastenings, touch-and-close tape

An appropriate loose cover can transform a relatively modern armchair or an old favourite armchair into a suitable piece for a period setting. Although the cover shown left is made as a loose cover with a tuck-in of fabric around the seat edge to hold the cover in place, it is in fact also secured to the chair with upholstery pins at a few points, to give a look that is halfway between a loose cover and an upholstered finish.

Armchairs come in so many shapes and sizes that you are almost bound to have to adapt the basic pattern in some way for your chair. For example, you might want a shallower valance, and you may need to make tucks or darts in the fabric for a smooth fit. However, the basic method of cutting out fabric rectangles for each section of the chair to be covered and fitting these in place over the chair with pins before stitching them together should apply. If your chair already has a loose cover, unpick it and use that as a pattern. The type of fabric you choose will largely depend on how much wear the chair will receive. For a favourite armchair choose a fairly heavyweight fabric; for an occasional chair you can buy a lighter weight fabric. Careful pattern matching is an essential ingredient to success. Work with the fabric right side out so that you can see the position of the pattern.

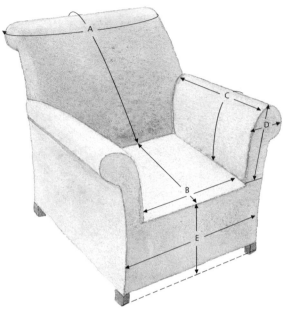

1 Start by carefully measuring each section of the chair, taking the maximum measurements lengthways and widthways.

A Inside back – from directly under the curve of the back of the chair over the top and down to the seat; across the inside back of the chair from side to side. Add on 15cm (6in) for a tuck-in at the back seat edge and 2cm (¾in) seam allowances on other edges.

B Seat – from the back to the front and from side to side, plus 15cm (6in) for tuck-ins at the back at each side and 2cm (¾in) for the front seam allowance.

C Inside arm (cut two) – from the seat over the top to underneath the curve of the arm, and from the outer back to the front of the arm. Add on 15cm (6in) for a tuck-in and 2cm (¾in) seam allowances on other edges.

D Front arm (cut two) – from the top of the arm down to the seat and widthways at the widest point, adding 2cm (¾in) seam allowances on all edges.

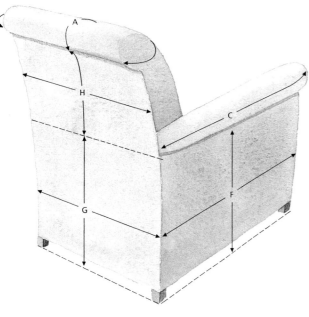

E Front valance – from the front edge of the seat to the floor and from side to side. Add 9.5cm (3¾in) to the finished depth for the seam allowance and hem, and 19cm (7½in) to the width (for the inverted pleats).
F Side valance (cut two) – from directly under the curve of the arm to the floor and from side to side, adding allowances as above.
G Back valance – from where the valance starts to the floor and from side to side, plus allowances as above.
H Outside back – from directly under the curve of the back to where the valance starts, plus 2cm (¾in) seam allowances on all edges.

For the inverted pleats cut out four pieces of fabric 19cm (7½in) wide – two to the depth of the front valance and two to the depth of the side valance.

For the cushion measure in the same way as for the day bed squab on page 84. If you wish to insert a zipper in the cushion, cut out the welt in four sections

(front, back and sides). The zipper is sewn in the back welt and it extends around the side edges to allow the pad to be easily inserted. Measure the length and depth of the back welt, adding 19cm (7½in) to the length and 6cm (2⅜in) to the depth for seams. For the front measure the length and depth and add 3cm (1¼in) all around for seams. For the sides deduct 5cm (2in) from the length and add 3cm (1¼in) to the depth. Allow extra fabric to make the piping to run around the top and bottom edges and around the front arm of the cushion.

2 To work out how much fabric you will require make a note of all the measurements, and then make a scale plan on graph paper. Draw each rectangle (two pieces when necessary – for example, two arms) to scale and cut them out. Next, draw two parallel lines on graph paper, set apart by the scale width of your chosen fabric. (The length of the lines will be a "guesstimate" of the length of fabric you require.) Mark any pattern repeat at intervals along the strip. Arrange the rectangles on the marked strip as close together as possible, keeping them square, and work out what length of fabric you require. Any large patterns or motifs will have to be centred on the main sections. Also make sure that any patterned or striped fabric flows in a continuous line from the top of the inside back down across the seat or cushion and down the front valance. The front arms should be cut so that the pattern will match the stripes on the front valance, while the side valance pieces should match up with the stripes on the arms and the back valance should match up with the outside back. After cutting out all the rectangles from fabric, label each piece on the back.

3 Take the seat piece and mark the centre front and back with pins and mark the same points on the chair seat. Smooth the fabric over the seat, matching pins and making sure that the grain is straight and the pattern is vertical. On the wrong side of the fabric mark the shape of the seat around the back and sides with tailor's chalk; trim to shape, leaving the 15cm (6in) tuck-in on the side and back edges and a 2cm (¾in) seam allowance at the the front edge. Tuck in the fabric at the back and sides.

4 Centre the inside back piece over the back of the chair. Bring the fabric over the top and pin in place directly under the curve of the back of the chair. At one side, tuck in the fabric between the inside back and the inside arm until you reach the stage where the tuck-in tapers out, mark this point on the wrong side of the fabric. Cut diagonally, almost to

this mark (if the angle is awkward pull the fabric out to do this). Smooth the fabric around the side and pin it in position down the back of the chair. With the fabric below the diagonal cut tucked-in, make a mark along the fold by pushing tailor's chalk or a pencil into the tuck. Pull the fabric back out and trim off any excess fabric to within 2cm (¾in) of the marked line, clipping into the fabric at regular intervals to make an even curve, then pin in position. Repeat this process at the other side of the chair.

a

b

5   Place one inside arm in position (a), folding the fabric back on itself at the back edge where the chair back and arm meet. Measure from the fold to the outside back edge of the chair, adding a 2cm (¾in) seam allowance. Trim the length to fit. Where the arm meets the inside back, until you reach the point where the tuck-in disappears, cut diagonally to this point, and trim to fit as with the inside back section. Pin to the inside back. Tuck the lower edge into

the seat and pin the outside edge in place underneath the curve of the arm. Pin the front arm in place (b). Trim to fit, leaving a 2cm (¾in) seam allowance all around. Repeat this process on the other arm.

6   Pin the outside back to the inside back along the top and at the sides. Leave the corners at this stage; they will be pleated and stitched later. Once the top half of the cover has been pinned to the chair check for fit. Before removing the cover from the chair open out the seams that have been pinned together and mark the stitching line with tailor's chalk. It is also useful to make lines across the seam at intervals so that you can match the points when you sew the cover.

7   Remove the top half of the chair's cover by unpinning one back side seam (the cover's opening). With right sides facing, repin the pieces

together, leaving the back side seam open, and adding covered piping cord between the inside arm and front arm (see page 148); then baste. Before machine-stitching the pieces together, turn the cover right side out and place on the chair to check for fit. Remove the cover from the chair. Oversew the edges of the back side opening to neaten. Sew touch and close tape down the opening side. Fold one side edge over 2cm (¾in) and pin one side of the touch-and-close tape to the underside, machine-stitch along both long edges and across the ends, leaving 1.5cm (¾in) at the bottom edges for seams. Pin the other half of the tape to the right side of the other edge. Check that the two halves line up correctly, then machine-stitch in place.

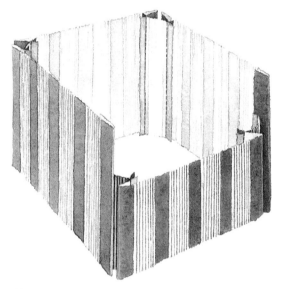

8   Next make up the valance. With right sides together and taking 2cm (¾in) seam allowances, pin and machine-stitch the valance pieces together. Join the side valance pieces to the front valance with short pleats in between and then join the back valance to the sides with long pleats in between.

9   Form the inverted pleats at each corner, with the seams at the back and making 7.5cm (3in) folds down each front edge.

10   Machine-stitch along the top to hold the inverted pleats in place, except on the back side seam that will be the opening side.

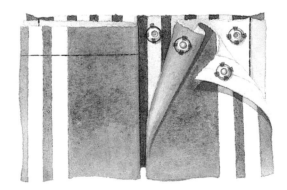

11   At the opening side, machine-stitch to hold one side of the inverted pleat only; at the other side, sew press studs or snap fastenings just within the seam allowance, to hold the pleat in place.

12   Next, with right sides together, pin and baste the valance to the top half of the cover, matching the chalk lines where they have been drawn. At the opening side, with the press studs or snap fastenings undone, pin and baste the front single layer of the valance (up to the fold) to one side of the back opening edge, leaving the back of the pleat free. Pin and baste the machined side of the pleat to the remaining back opening. Neaten the top edges of the valance by oversewing. Place the cover over the chair once again and check for fit and that the pattern matches up correctly. Pin the bottom edge of the valance under 2.5cm (1in) and then 5cm (2in), adjusting this allowance if necessary. When you are satisfied with the fit remove the cover and machine-stitch the valance to the cover and hem the bottom edge.

13   Place the cover on the chair, and decide exactly where the rosettes are to go. At the top of each side lightly hammer an upholstery tack into the centre of the place chosen for the rosette or covered button, to act as a marker. Gradually, pull the fabric over the tack, and mark the point where each fold or pleat of fabric touches the tack with tailor's chalk. When you have done this at each side, take the cover off the chair and remove the upholstery tacks. Using strong thread and taking fairly long stitches run a gathering thread around the marked points. Pull the gathering thread taut and tie it off; trim the seam allowance to reduce bulk. Replace the cover over the chair and, make any adjustments necessary to the gathers for a good finished appearance. Secure the gathers with a few stitches (these will be covered by the rosette or covered button). Firmly hammer an upholstery tack into

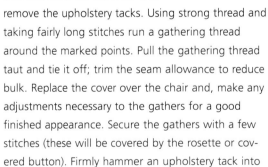

the chair through the centre of the gathered corner, then slipstitch a rosette or covered button to cover the tack and the gathering stitches.

14   For the cushion, cover sufficient piping cord with matching fabric cut on the bias to go around the top and base (see page 148). To insert a zipper in the cushion cut the back welt in half lengthways. With right sides together, taking a 1.5cm (⅝in) seam allowance, machine-stitch about 2.5cm (1in) in from each end, leaving an opening for the zipper in the middle. Insert the zipper down the middle before joining the back welt to the rest of the welt. Next add the piping cord. Starting at the middle of the back edge, pin and machine-stitch the piping cord around the right side of the top and base pieces, with the cord facing inward and the raw edges together. Once the piping is in place, sew the welt to the top and base in the same way as for the day bed squab on page 84, making sure that the zipper is at the back and the seams of the welt are at the sides.

Buttoned treatments

The heyday of buttoning, or *le style capitonné*, came during the middle of the 19th century, although it evolved from the 18th-century technique of float-tufting. This was a means of securing the stuffing inside squabs (seat-pads), and involved looping a series of linen threads passed through the upholstery around a small bunch of silk or linen fibres. The latter formed tufts that sat tight on the surface of the squabs.

Tufting was initially used in France around 1720, on squabs tied to the seats and backs of cane chairs. In the second half of the 18th century, in Britain, America and Sweden, tufting was also used on chairs, benches and day-beds with fixed upholstery. By about 1840, the development of springing and a fashion of ever-thicker layers of stuffing rendered tufting obsolete. A stronger method was required to take the greater strains imposed, and buttons provided the means.

The technique of deep-buttoning changed the shape of seating by accentuating the thickness and curvaceousness of upholstery – resulting in the heavily stuffed, deeply buttoned and elaborately trimmed chairs, sofas, ottomans and pouffes that dominated Victorian interiors between 1845 and 1875.

Deep-buttoning gradually went out of fashion in the late 1880s, in a general reaction to the over-fussiness of upholstery styles during the previous four-and-a-half decades.

Right: *A deep-buttoned, silk damask covered, Victorian "conversation settee", Natchez, Mississippi, USA.*

Right: *A deep-buttoned armchair from a Rococo-revival parlour suite made in Philadelphia, USA. The suite was listed in an inventory of the Melrose Mansion, Natchez, Mississippi, USA, completed in 1865. It was recovered during the 1940s with a fabric similar to the original.*

Far right: *A Victorian button-back sofa covered in silk damask, and a nursing chair covered in a deep-pile velvet.*

Below right: *A reproduction Victorian, deep-buttoned, faded chintz sofa, made by George Smith of London.*

Below: *A fine-quality, 19th-century settee, recovered in a Scalamandré documentary fabric, in the Owens Thomas House, Savannah, Georgia, USA.*

99

Bed treatments

Prior to the 18th century, the bed was the most prized possession in the majority of households, and its hangings invariably the most valuable. This is no surprise when you take into account the fact that beds then were generally larger than they are now. For example, it was said that on the Great Bed of Ware (1580), in England, "four couples might cosily lie side by side, and thus without touching each other abide". Indeed, it was reckoned that some 46 metres (50 yards) of fabric was required to make hangings for a relatively insignificant single bed. During the 19th and 20th centuries, beds became smaller and less ornate, and it is unlikely that the twelve-year commission Louis XIV of France offered to master embroiderer Delobel to make the bed-hangings at Versailles will ever be matched again.

Above & Right: *A bedroom in a medieval town-house in Monflanquin, France, boasts a late 19th-century, distressed-painted brass and iron bed. The embroidered quilt with red and beige flower motifs is also late 19th century. The printed cotton sheets, embroidered linen pillowcases and the muslin mosquito net are modern.*

Four-posters

Four-poster beds with ornate fabric canopies appeared during the 15th century, and became larger and more elaborate over the next hundred years. Wealthier householders had woven silk bed-hangings, trimmed with gold and silver lace fringe and topped with satin canopies. The less affluent managed with hangings of wool and linen (sometimes painted to resemble tapestry).

During the 17th century, hangings for four-posters became increasingly sophisticated, with canopies of pelmeted and fringed hangings sometimes rising into domes. Favoured fabrics included tapestries, damasks, brocades, watered-silks, taffetas and moirés. Moreover, the four-poster began to look less like an enclosed box. Upper frames were carved and descending hangings lighter, often raised in festoons rather than drawn. Many pelmets and valances were embroidered and bordered with silks, and hangings appliquéd with fashionable motifs.

Although four-posters were increasingly replaced by half-testers (see pages 114–15)

and *à la duchesse* beds during the latter part of the 17th century – and *polonaise* and "Turkish" beds during the 18th century – they were still much in evidence until the 1740s, particularly in England and America. Under the influence of Rococo and Palladian styles, they became even lighter in appearance – partly because imported cotton chintzes from India and painted silks from the Far East were often used for hangings.

Although four-posters became unfashionable during the latter half of the 18th and early 19th centuries, they enjoyed a revival at the start of the Victorian era. Canopied four-posters, with hangings to match the window drapes, were a feature of early Victorian bedrooms. The preoccupation with hygiene resulted in a near-terminal decline during the latter part of the 19th century. For example, the influential designer and critic Charles Eastlake felt it was healthier to sleep on beds with no hangings at all, except in humid climes where nets could be hung from the posts to protect against mosquitoes.

Far left: *A modern pine four-poster bed, in a 16th-century French manoir. The pelmet and printed bed-hangings are cotton. The hand-stitched, embroidered quilt is 19th century.*

Left: *A four-poster with 18th-century toile bed canopy and drapes. The bolster and over-quilt are covered in modern, checked Perigord fabrics.*

Right: *Although modern, the checked Perigord fabric covering the bed quilt is in a design which has been produced since the 18th century.*

Left & Below: *The 19th-century mahogany four-poster bed in a Greek-revival house in Charleston, USA, has been left undraped. The light and airy feel to the room is further augmented by a combination of embroidered-linen pillow-cases and a 19th-century embroidered-lace bedcover. The drapes, or sheers, are made to an early 19th-century design from silk organza – which was a fabric primarily used for ladies' petticoats.*

Below: *The Jacobean bedroom in the Calhoun mansion, in Charleston, South Carolina, USA, includes a fine four-poster dating, in part, to 1660 and featuring carving and marquetry inlay. The bed-hangings are modern tapestry, but in period style. The bedspread is a plain green cotton lawn.*

Above: *The headboard and sections of the valances (top and bottom) of this 19th-century four-poster in a French hunting lodge are covered in pieces of 19th-century silk. These were salvaged from a larger piece of badly worn material bought by the current owners of the lodge. The rest of the hangings, including the back curtain and inner valance, are made from a modern bale silk.*

Right: *A 19th-century tapestry, depicting mythological scenes, hangs on the wall above the headboard of a fruit-wood four-poster in a bedroom of a French hunting lodge.*

Above: *A magnificent Regency four-poster, with its original red silk damask hangings, in the Prince's Room at Temple Newsam house, in England.*

Right: *In a bedroom at Green Leaves, a Greek-revival house in Natchez, Mississippi, USA, the mid-19th-century four-poster has been re-upholstered in a modern silk that is an exact copy of its original fabric. The brass rosette is period.*

Above & Right: *A late 18th-century four-poster, with modern chintz hangings, in an English manor house. The bedspread is a modern copy of a Victorian quilt.*

Below & Below right: *Watered-silk drapes, a tapestry pelmet or cornice and old Battenburg lace (see bedspread) enhance a "four-leaf clover", or "Four Apostle", bed.*

Left & Far left: *An early 15th-century four-poster in the Walnut Bedroom at Leeds Castle, Kent, England. The bed-hangings and quilt have been restored, and are a mixture of predominantly English and, to a lesser extent, French embroidery. The elaborate and finely worked floral motifs are typical of the period. Initial restoration of the room took place in the 1930s.*

Below left & Far left: *The four-poster in the Green Bedroom at Leeds Castle was made in Spain during the 17th century. The silk appliqué bed-hangings feature foliage motifs and strapwork of Moorish design and are almost certainly original to the bed.*

Below right & Opposite: *A magnificent medieval pastiche, also at Leeds Castle. The bed-hangings, and the throw over the side-chair, are monogrammed silk.*

Left: *The master bedroom of Cedar Grove, Vicksburg, Mississippi, USA, decorated in fashionable 1840s shades of lilac and yellow. The swagged silk hangings on the four-poster are embellished with "campaign" fringing.*

Right: *The swag-and-tail hangings on this American four-poster (made by Prudent Mallard of New Orleans) are copies of a documentary 1850s fabric.*

Far right: *An early 19th-century, American Federal-style bed with a swagged chintz pelmet and chintz bedspread.*

Above: *When this four-poster in an 1830s New York house was restored, enough of the original red silk damask fabric was found in the frame to enable an accurate restoration.*

Right: *The General Quitman bedroom in the Monmouth mansion, Natchez, Mississippi, USA, has been restored in a late-1820s style. Swagged drapes and hangings are velvet.*

Dressing a four-poster

Above: *This four-poster has been created from a divan, using floor-to-ceiling posts, lengths of moulding and masses of fabric, tassels, bows and braids.*

MATERIALS

- Basic sewing kit (see page 146)
- Main fabric
- Contrast fabric (for curtain lining)
- Interlining
- Fringing
- Paper and pencil for pattern
- Net (for stiffening bows)
- Glue (and glue gun – optional, but useful for gluing fringing and other trimmings in place)
- Fabric-covered buttons (kits to make these are available from most haberdashery stores)
- Touch-and-close tape
- Four-poster bed or frame and curtain trackining

This lavishly decorated four-poster is a highly individual interpretation of the grand Empire style. The treatment for a four-poster depends on the structure of the frame, and this will vary with each individual bed. Modern examples may have wooden or metal frames, and the curtain tracking may be concealed under or on the inside of the bars. A canopy similar to the one featured here could, in fact, be suspended from the ceiling joists, making posts superfluous and enabling the curtain tracking to run all around the inner frame. However, if you want to construct a four-poster, it is better to have a frame around the bed at a lower level (say, in line with the bottom of the mattress), as well as at the upper level, rather than attempting to fix the posts to the bed itself. Another option – used to make the bed seen here – is to secure the posts to the floor and the ceiling. Once the drapes and pelmet or cornice have been made, the bed can be further embellished with a wide range of trimmings.

Drapes

The curtain requirements will vary according to the construction of the bed. In general, four-poster curtains are designed for show rather than practical use, so they do not need to be very full. The curtain tape is normally placed on the outward-facing side of the curtains (see pages 116 and 122), where it will be concealed by the pelmet or cornice. In this treatment fringing decorates the hem of the curtains.

Pelmet or cornice and ceiling

Use interlining to slightly stiffen the pelmet or cornice, as for the pelmet or cornice on page 22. Make the lining from the main or a contrasting fabric to match the curtains. Attach the pelmet or cornice to the frame with touch-and-close tape, for a neat finish. If the curtain tracks are visible from the inside of the bed, they can be concealed behind an inner valance. The ceiling of a four-poster is often covered with fabric, attached either to a solid frame or cross bars. The fabric can be arranged in several ways; for example, pleated up to a central point, with raw edges turned under and stapled in place, then covered with braid.

Pipes

The pipe on the four-poster is placed on the pelmet or cornice with a rosette positioned at the top. You can make two different-shaped pipes from one pattern. To make a pattern, start with a rectangle measuring the finished depth by twice the finished width (at its widest point). Draw a gentle curve upward along the bottom edge. At the top of the rectangle draw a line (centred) measuring just over half the bottom line. Then draw the sides by joining the top and bottom

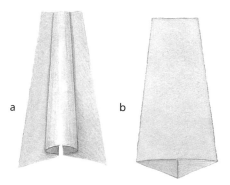

lines together. Cut out 2 pieces of main fabric, adding 1.5cm (⅝in) all around. At the top edge press over the seam allowance to the wrong side. With right sides together, machine-stitch the two pieces together along the side and bottom edges. Turn right side out, press and slipstitch the top folded edges together. Hand sew fringing along the bottom hem, if required. For the left-hand pipe form the inverted pleat at the top (a), pin and machine-stitch to hold. For the right-hand pipe fold the pipe so that the two edges meet down the middle of the back. Press and slipstitch the seam (b).

Rosettes

To make a rosette, cut out a strip of main or contrast fabric measuring 7.5 x 70cm (3 x 28in). With right sides together, join the two short edges, taking a 12mm (½in) seam allowance. Press the seam open and then, with wrong sides together, fold the circular strip in half, bringing the raw edges together. Run a

gathering thread though both thicknesses, 6 mm (¼in) in from the raw edge (a). Pull the gathering thread, drawing the fabric into a tight circle, and finish with a few stitches. Sew a fabric-covered button in the middle of the rosette to cover the raw edges (b).

Bow

Easy to make, bows can be used to decorate pelmets or cornices, as well as for curtain tie-backs.

1 To make a bow, cut out a piece of main fabric and net (for stiffening), measuring 21.5 x 42cm (8½ x 16½in). Place the net on the wrong side of the main fabric and with right sides facing fold the length of the fabric and net in half lengthways. Pin and then machine-stitch, taking a 12mm (½in) seam allowance. Press the seam open. Turn the tube right side out, and press flat, so that the seam runs down the middle at the back. With the right sides facing, pin and machine-stitch the short edges together, taking a 12mm (½in) seam allowance. Press the seam open, and turn the tube right side out – see (b) below.

2 Cut a strip of main fabric measuring 4 x 13cm (1½ x 5in). Fold the long raw edges in to meet down the centre on the wrong side (a). With the joining seam at the inside back, flatten the fabric tube made above (b) and pinch it into an inverted pleat at

the centre (c); wrap the short strip around the pleated centre of the tube, and stitch in place at the back, trimming away any excess fabric (d).

3 For the tails of the bow, cut two strips of fabric, each measuring 14 x 42.5cm (5½ x 16in). With right sides 'together, take each strip and fold it in half lengthways, then stitch down the long side, angling it at the end to make a point (a). Trim; turn right side out, and press. Position the two prepared strips so that the raw edges overlap and stitch to the back of the bow (b).

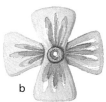

Maltese cross

To make a Maltese cross – a variation of a bow – sew two fabric tubes (stiffened with net) as described in Bow step 1. Pinch one tube into a bow shape (a) and stitch to secure the shape, then put this inside the second tube, placing the two at right angles to each other. Pinch the front and back of the second tube individually, then sew a covered button to the middle of the cross.

Half-testers

Half-testers came to prominence during the 17th century. Strictly speaking, they had two headposts and no endposts, with their canopies suspended above the middle or toward the end of the bed from ropes attached to the ceiling. Originating in France as *lits à la duchesse*, they featured decorative valances and hangings often *en-suite* with other furnishings. In fact, many half-testers were *lits d'ange* (or *lits à l'impériale*): postless beds with "flying" canopies suspended from the wall behind the bedhead.

Developments during the 18th century included a shortening of the hangings, and/or the inclusion of cords and rings which allowed the drapes to be pulled up into festoons. Scalloped valances also became fashionable and

hangings were generally lighter. They were often in silk or block-printed cottons, and featured Oriental and Egyptian motifs.

During the second half of the 19th century, the half-tester (or Arabian bed as it became known in England) was promoted over the four-poster for reasons of health and hygiene – offering better air circulation, less dust and fewer bedbugs. The popularity of such beds was reflected in Queen Victoria's choice of one with chintz hangings in her bedroom at Balmoral. F. Heal & Son's catalogue of 1880 showed over 12 different ways to drape a half-tester, and incorporated a wide range of appropriate draperies and bedding – including mosquito netting for army officers overseas.

Above: *This Victorian pastiche of a half-tester is in the bedroom of a London townhouse. The bed has no posts at all, and the Italian carved wooden canopy extends barely any distance from the wall (to which it is secured). Strictly speaking, this is a "flying" canopy and the bed a lit d'ange. The swag-and-tail brown silk hangings complement the "panther velour" bedspread (animal-skin coverings were much in vogue during the latter half of the 19th century).*

Left: *A fine example of a carved rosewood and walnut half-tester, in 19th-century Renaissance-revival style, at the Garth Woodside Mansion, Hannibal, Missouri, USA. The drapes and bedding are modern, machine-made, period-style lace.*

Right: *A mid-century Prudent Mallard half-tester in the Monmouth Mansion, in Natchez, Mississippi, USA. The swagged silk damask hangings are modern, but are copied from documentary prints of the 19th century.*

Below: *Another Prudent Mallard half-tester c.1850, in the New Orleans bedroom at the American Museum in Bath, England. The heaviness of the carved mahogany is offset by the use of muslin and lace hangings.*

Creating a half-tester

MATERIALS

- ◆ Basic sewing kit (see page 146)
- ◆ Curtain fabric
- ◆ Braid
- ◆ Standard heading tape for curtains
- ◆ Pencil-pleated heading tape for valance
- ◆ Pinking shears
- ◆ Curtain hooks
- ◆ Curtain wire and fixings
- ◆ Tester board and brackets
- ◆ Screw eyes
- ◆ Fabric glue or stapel gun
- ◆ Cord and tassel tie-backs and hooks

A half-tester creates an effect similar to a four-poster bed, but it is effectively a wide valanced pelmet or cornice with matching drapes, very similar to the curtains on page 46, but arranged to frame the head of a bed rather than a window. The treatment can look effective in a wide range of fabrics and trims: for example, the drapes and pelmet might be of rich, heavy velvet, with a matching lining and bullion fringing, but for the very frilled and ruffled look featured here choose a light fabric, such as cotton lawn, silk or organdie. The drapes are very full and unlined, to maintain the light, feminine atmosphere. The height of a half-tester is usually determined by the height of the curtain treatment in the room.

Left: *The fabric used in this half-tester is silk which hangs beautifully in this elaborate treatment. The ruffles are extremely full and the edges have been cleverly pinked, adding to the lavish effect.*

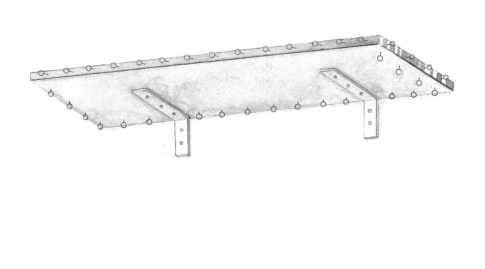

1 The tester board should be the same width as the bed, about 35cm (14in) deep and can be made from 2cm (¾in) thick wood. Using fabric glue or a staple gun, cover the underside of the board with curtain fabric (if the fabric is very fine, you may wish to cover the board first with a plain cotton and then with the curtain fabric). The curtains are attached to screw eyes, fixed under the tester board, and the valance is attached to screw eyes fixed to the edge of the tester board. Secure it to the wall with brackets.

2 For these very full unlined drapes you will require 2½ to 3 times the finished width of the sides and back of the tester board. Make the side curtains about 38cm (15in) longer than the board to floor measurement to allow for the sides to be draped with tie-backs and for the hems. The flounce on each side is made from one long strip of fabric, measuring about 7.5cm (3in) wide by 2½ times the length of the leading edge. For pinked flounces cut out one straight edge and pink one edge. For the back curtain measure from the tester board to the top of the skirting or base board plus 7.5cm (3in) for turning over at the top and a casing at the bottom edge for curtain wire – this is attached to screw eyes in the top of the skirting or base board and holds the curtain in place.

3 To make the valance you will need a piece of fabric 2½ to 3 times the combined length of the width and sides of the tester board by about 25.5cm (10in). The valance is lined with the curtain fabric so cut out two sections. Cut and join strips for the flounce as above, making the total length 2½ times the length of the valance.

4 To prepare the flounces join the strips of fabric with French seams (see page 148). If you have not pinked the edges make a narrow, double 6mm (¼in) hem along the long edge of both flounces. Also make narrow double hems at each end. Run two parallel lines of gathering along the remaining long edge of each ruffle, one on the seam line and the second just within the 1.5cm (⅝in) seam allowance.

5 Join any side curtain widths with French seams (see page 148). Gather the flounce to fit the leading edge, starting 2.5cm (1in) down from the raw edge at the top and finishing 15cm  (6in) up from the raw edge at the bottom. With right sides facing, pin in place, taking a 1.5cm (⅝in) seam allowance and then machine-stitch.

6 Press the right side of the flounce toward the leading edge with the seam facing inward. Pin the braid in position on the right side of the fabric next to the flounce. With matching thread, machine- or hand-stitch the braid in place, sewing through all thicknesses so as to hold the seam in place. To finish, cover the raw edges at the back by neatly hand-stitching either braid, matching seam binding or ribbon first to the flounce and then to the curtain.

7 Turn over and machine-stitch a double 2.5cm (1in) hem down the other side edge. Turn up a double 7.5cm (3in) hem at the bottom and stitch by hand. Repeat the process for the other side curtain.

8 At the top of each side curtain, turn the raw edge over to the right side to a depth of 4cm (1in). Attach the heading tape (see page 48) on this side, setting the top edge of the tape just below the foldline, so that the hooks and tape will not be seen from the bed and will be concealed at the front by the valance. Gather the side curtains, insert curtain hooks in the tape and attach to the screw eyes.

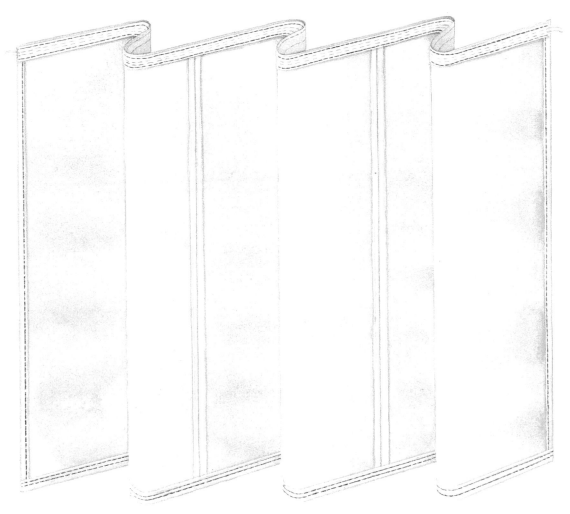

10 For the valance, gather the flounce and attach it to the valance in the same way as in step 5. In this case the flounce should start and finish 1.5cm (⅝in) short of the raw side edges (so that the flounce does not get in the way of the lining). Attach the braid to the right side of the valance next to the flounce in the same way as in step 6.

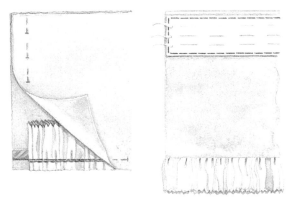

11 With right sides together, the flounce lying inward and taking a 1.5cm (⅝in) seam allowance, pin and then machine-stitch the valance lining to the main outer piece down the sides and along the lower edge. Turn right side out and turn both raw top edges over to the lining side, making a 2.5cm (1in) fold. Pin and machine-stitch the pencil pleat heading tape in place along the top edge. Gather the valance, and secure it to the screw eyes in the pelmet board with curtain hooks.

9 For the back curtain, taking a 1.5cm (⅝in) seam allowance and with right sides facing, machine-stitch the fabric widths together. Press the seams flat. Turn over and machine-stitch a double 2.5cm (1in) hem down each side edge. At the top edge press over a 2.5cm (1in) turning to the wrong side. Next pin the heading tape in position just below the fold at the top and machine-stitch. For the casing at the bottom edge, turn up a double 2.5cm (1in) hem to the wrong side. Machine-stitch the hem close to the folded edge, and then stitch a second, parallel line, 12mm (½in) below the first. Gather the back curtain, and insert curtain hooks in the tape. Attach to the screw eyes at the top. At the bottom edge thread curtain wire through the casing and secure the gathered curtain to screw eyes fixed in the skirting or base board.

12 Fix hooks for the tie-backs to the wall at each side of the bed. Loop tie-backs around the side curtains. If there are any gaps between the back and side curtains, hand-stitch the sides from the top down to a point just above the tie-backs.

Corona style

During the Middle Ages, many domestic beds were styled on those used during military campaigns. A typical early arrangement involved placing the bedstead under a tented, striped canopy hung from a crown or ring (a corona) suspended either from the ceiling or the wall behind the head of the bed.

Coronas have provided an alternative to bedposts as a means of supporting bed-hangings ever since – particularly where a domed, rather than a flat, canopy or tester was required. Thus, some 18th-century *lits à la polonaise* featured a fabric dome built around a concealed corona secured by curved rods attached to the four corners of the bedstead.

During the 19th century, the majority of coronas were on show and attached to the wall or ceiling. For example, beds placed side-on against the wall, in the French style, often had draperies trailing over their ends from wall-mounted and ornamented wooden or metal coronas. Ceiling-mounted coronas, often simple steel or brass rings, were also much in evidence where mosquito netting and muslin and lace sheers were draped over the bed.

Opposite: *A lit bateau, probably used by Napoleon when he was First Consul of the French Republic, in the Morris Jumel Mansion, New York, USA. The fringed silk drapes swagged on the wall add to a lit à la Turque arrangement.*

Right: *Muslin drapes hang from a corona-style fixture above a bed in a medieval French townhouse.*

Below middle & Right: *Simple corona-style fittings and mosquito nets trimmed with gold braid, above a pair of beds in a Charleston townhouse, South Carolina, USA.*

Below left: *A carved and gilt-wood corona. The wreaths and other foliate motifs are classically inspired.*

Making a corona

MATERIALS

- Basic sewing kit (see page 146)
- Main fabric
- Inner (lining) fabric
- Curtain heading tape
- Curtain hooks
- Braid
- Buckram
- Hooks and eyes
- Piece of 2cm (¾in) thick blockboard and fixings (screws for coronas attached to the ceiling, angle brackets and screws for wall-mounted coronas)
- Saw or jigsaw and sandpaper
- Staple gun with staples, or fabric adhesive
- Screw eyes, nails and small curtain rings or touch-and-close tape

Left: *A lit à la Turque arrangement in which the corona and hangings are matched with the walls and head- and foot-boards of the bed, creating a striking visual impact. In this treatment the vivid and colourful fabric predominates so the design of the pelmet or cornice does not need to be too elaborate, hence this pelmet or cornice is pleated and has braid attached to the top and bottom edges.*

Extremely elegant, a corona is a variation on the half-tester, with two side curtains and a back curtain. The side curtains are made somewhat longer than the back one. This allows for the effect of tie-backs or, as here, means that the curtains can be draped over the ends of the bed. The inner fabric for the corona drapes should be the same weight as the main fabric. Choose either the same or a plain or less emphatically patterned design, as in the photograph. Corona boards can be attached to the wall with angle brackets or screwed to joists in the ceiling. The wall-attached variety is often semi-circular and referred to as a half-corona. Flexible curtain tracking can be curved into a relatively small circle and fixed to the board. However, because the curtains do not need to be pulled back they can be suspended from permanent fixings, such as screw eyes. It is relatively simple to make (or have made) your own corona board, the essential thing being to make sure that it is very securely fixed. It is also possible to buy corona kits from specialist interior design shops and some department stores.

1   The corona shown left is attached to the ceiling and is not circular but an oval shape. This style could also be used at the head of a double bed, since the curtains hang over the length of a single bed. The circumference of the corona should be approximately 140cm (55in). A half-corona for a single bed would be about 50cm (20in) across at the back and 22cm (9in) deep, and for a double bed about 60cm (23½in) at the back by 30cm (12in) deep. Mark and cut out with a saw or jigsaw your circle, oval or semi-circle on the wood or blockboard/wood. Smooth the edges with sandpaper.

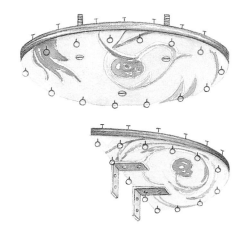

2   Using the blockboard as a pattern, cut out a piece of fabric to cover the underside of the board, adding an extra 1.3cm (½in) all around to turn the raw edges under. Staple or glue fabric to the underside of the board. On the fabric-covered side of the board insert screw eyes around the edge; place nails around the top edge of the board (or attach one side of the touch-and-close tape along the front of the edge). Secure your board to the ceiling joists with 5cm (2in) screws. To attach the corona to the wall, decide on the height above the bed, say about 220cm (7ft), and secure in place with brackets.

3   In general, for a single bed, you will require 1½ widths for each side curtain and 1½ widths for the back curtain; for a double bed, 2 widths for each side curtain and 2 widths for the back curtain. For the treatment featured here, make as for a double bed (2 widths for each side curtain and 2 widths for the back curtain), to allow for the bed being set lengthways. To estimate how much main fabric is required, measure from the board to the desired finished length adding 17.5cm (7in) for the heading and hem. For the inner

curtains allow 7.5cm (3in) for the heading and hem and trim the leading edge of each side curtain by 5cm (2in). When the outer and inner curtains are joined together, the main fabric will show at the leading edge and hem. The back curtain for a half-corona will lie flat against the wall and can, therefore, be made as an unlined curtain from the inner fabric only (see page 67). If your fabric is patterned, you must allow for pattern repeats (see pages 149–50).

4   To make the side curtains, with right sides facing, matching any pattern and taking 12mm (½)in seam allowances, join the outer and inner fabric widths together. Press the seams open. For each side curtain, with right sides facing and side and top edges matching, place the inner fabric on top of the outer fabric. Taking a 1.5cm (⅝in) seam allowance, starting 2.5cm (1in) below the top edge and stopping 5cm (2in) above the lower edge of the inner fabric – leaving 12.5cm (5in) of main fabric showing – pin and machine-stitch the side seams. Either remove selvedges or cut notches into the seam allowance, to avoid pulling.

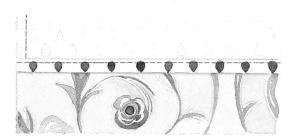

5   On the wrong side of the inner fabric, turn up and press a double 2.5cm (1in) hem and then machine-stitch.

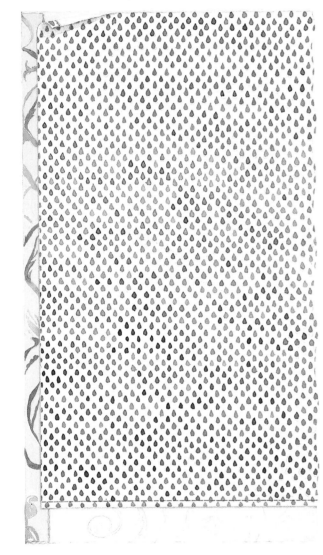

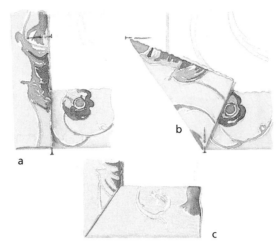

a

b

c

9   Along the top edge, fold the main fabric over to the wrong side making a 2.5cm (1in) turning, press. Bring 2.5cm (1in) of the inner fabric over the folded edge of the main fabric, press.

7   Before hemming the side curtains, you will need to mitre the leading edge corners. Turn up and press a double 7.5cm (3in) hem to the wrong side of the main fabric. Press over the leading side edge. Place a pin where the bottom hem finishes (a). Place a second pin at the bottom edge where the side hem finishes (b). Open out the side hem and then open out the first 7.5cm (3in) of the bottom hem; fold the fabric along a line between these two pins. Press over the side seam and turn up the bottom edge, making a double 7.5cm (3in) hem. Baste the hem.

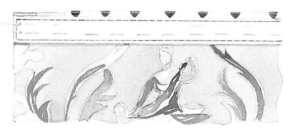

10   Pin the heading tape in place, covering the raw edge and setting the tape close to the folded edge. Fold in the edges of the heading tape at each side and, making sure that the drawing cords are clear of all stitching, machine-stitch the tape in place along its top, bottom and side edges.

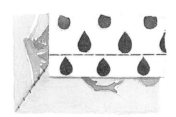

6   Turn the curtain right side out. Press the side seams so that there is a 5cm (2in) border of main fabric showing on the leading edge. Press the other side flat so that neither the main or inner fabric shows on the other side.

8   Slipstitch the mitre folds, the hem and the inner and outer fabrics together at the bottom edge, then remove the basting stitches.

11   For the back curtain, join the main and inner widths of fabric. Press the seams flat. Place the inner fabric on top of the outer fabric, right sides facing and with top and side edges matching, and machine-stitch the side seams in the same way as for the side curtains. Turn the back curtain right side out and press the side edges flat.

12 Turn up and machine-stitch a double
2.5cm (1in) hem along the lower edge of
the inner fabric. It will not be necessary to mitre the
corners of the hem because the back curtain has no
leading edge. Along the lower edge of the main fabric turn up and handstitch a double 7.5cm (3in) hem.
At the top edge, fold over 2.5cm (1in) of main fabric
to the wrong side. Bring 2.5cm (1in) of inner fabric
over the folded edge of the outer fabric and attach
heading tape as for the side curtains.

13 The finished curtains should look like one
curtain. If necessary, sew hooks and eyes
at intervals to the side edges of the back curtain and
the inner side edges of the side curtains, so that they
are held together from the corona board down to
bed height.

14 Gather the heading tape to fit the circumference of the corona board. Insert curtain
hooks in the tape and attach the curtains to the
screw eyes fixed in the corona board.

15 For the pleated pelmet or cornice you will
need a piece of fabric three times the
circumference of the corona board (or the front,
curved edge, for half-coronas) by the required depth
of the pelmet or cornice, about 15cm (6in), plus
1.5cm (⅝in) all around for seams. The inner fabric
should be the circumference of the corona (or the
front, curved edge, if you are making a half-corona)
by the same depth as the main fabric, plus 1.5cm
(⅝in) all around for seams. Cut out a piece of buckram
to the same size as the lining, less seam allowances.

16 Make the pleats in the main pelmet
or cornice fabric (use the photograph
as a guide to the size of the pleats). Pin in place
and then machine-stitch along the top and
bottom edges.

17 Using herringbone stitch, attach the buckram to the back of the pelmet or cornice
(see page 49). Next, turn the pleated seam allowances
to the wrong side over the buckram and baste to hold.

18 On the right side hand- or machine-stitch
the braid in place along the top and
bottom edges, sewing through all thicknesses.

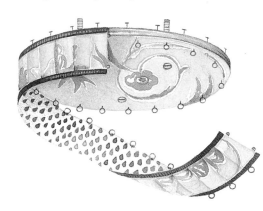

19 Turn in the seam allowances, 1.5cm (⅝in),
on all edges of the inner lining section.
Slipstitch this to the wrong side of the main section,
covering all raw edges. Sew small curtain rings along
the top edge of the pelmet or cornice to correspond
with the nails in the board. Or, if you are using touch-
and-close tape, hand sew the hooked side to the top
edge of the pelmet. Lastly, sew hooks and eyes to the
short edges of the pelmet to close.

Standard beds

Prior to the middle of the 18th century, beds neither fully or partly enclosed by hangings were a rarity for all but the servants of a household. However, the rise of the cabinet-maker and carver, in combination with improved insulation of windows and doors, gradually diminished the importance of bed-hangings.

The bedstead came out into the open increasingly during the 19th century, and was topped and tailed with carved and/or painted wooden head- and footboards. Favoured hardwoods included mahogany, rosewood and walnut. However, oak, satinwood and bamboo were also popular – while softwoods, such as pine, were usually flat-painted and sometimes embellished with decorative motifs.

The opening-up of beds was further fuelled by 19th-century concerns for health and hygiene. Fewer or no hangings meant less dust and better circulation of air – factors which also contributed to the popularity of the iron and brass bedsteads produced in vast numbers during the last quarter of the 19th century. Not surprisingly, these developments in turn resulted in a greater emphasis on the decorative role of bed linen, quilts and counterpanes.

Above: *Antique linen and lace on a 19th-century painted cast-iron bed in an 18th-century London townhouse.*

Left & Far left: *A 19th-century painted iron cot dressed in gingham, plus a French quilt and English wool blanket.*

Below & Opposite: *A modern Indian copy of an 18th-century Aubusson rug on a 19th-century brass and iron bed.*

Far left: *A simple bed dressed with embroidered linen and a floral Mercella bedcover from the 1850s. The bedside table is covered with a silk embroidered shawl c.1900.*

Left: *Modern cotton toiles and checks combine happily with painted wooden and cane bedheads in a Norfolk manor house, England.*

Below right & Opposite: *In a château on the Dordogne, France, an 18th-century, painted and gilded country bed is still embellished with its original toile inserts on the head- and footboard.*

Above: *Early 19th-century chintz from the Auvergne is used as a bedspread and covering for the sofa in a mid-19th-century manoir on the Dordogne, France.*

Right: *A painted wooden country bed with a late 19th-century cotton bedspread and embroidered bed linen.*

Quilts

Decorative quilts, made of fabrics as diverse as figured silk, damask, chintz and *toiles de Jouy*, fall into three main categories. Each is based on a different method of manufacture – although the techniques were sometimes combined.

Traditional quilting involves backing a fabric with padding and underlining, and stitching a pattern through the layers. Quilts of this type were popular in Britain and America during the 18th and 19th centuries. A variant, Trapunto quilting, incorporates areas of sculptured relief. It was also fashionable in 17th- and 18th-century Europe and 19th-century America.

Appliquéd quilts are made by stitching pieces of cloth and other decorative objects, such as beads, over a plain ground. Typical motifs include flowers, fruit, leaves, birds, animals and people, while designs are often pictorial representations of important events. Appliquéd quilts were used throughout Europe during the 16th and 17th centuries, and were also produced in America (notably Pennsylvania) from the 18th century onward.

Patchwork quilts have no groundcloth and are made by stitching pieces of different fabrics together to form an overall pattern. Some feature a central medallion surrounded by plain or patterned borders. However, most patterns are geometric mosaics of shapes such as diamonds or stars. The majority of patchwork quilts were made in America during the 19th century, notably among the Amish communities.

Opposite & Left: *A late 19th-century hand-stitched "boutie". Another sits on the 19th-century cane-panelled chair.*

Below: *A selection of brightly coloured, traditionally patterned, Provençal quilts, from France.*

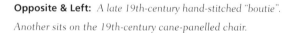

Top: *A 19th-century ladderback chair with a "crazy" quilt and matching teddy, made c.1880 in Pennsylvania, USA.*

Above: *A "Whig's Defeat" quilt on a traditional "cannon-ball" bed in Tullie Smith House, Atlanta, Georgia, USA.*

131

Accessories

The use to which fabrics have been put in the home extends beyond the covering and draping of windows, walls, floors, doors, beds and upholstered seating. All manner of materials have been pressed into service to provide protection as well as colour, pattern and texture to a range of other surfaces and objects. Dining tables, occasional tables, dressing tables, cushions or pillows, shelves, screens and lamps have all been dressed to play their part in decorative room schemes. The extent to which they have been draped, covered and trimmed has invariably been a matter of fashion. For example, the relatively restrained application of fabrics in both English Georgian and American Shaker interiors contrasts strongly with the almost profligate use of them during the great Victorian "cover-up" of the 19th century.

Above & Right: *A traditional blue-and-white check linen tablecloth in the dining room of a 17th-century French château on the Dordogne. The faïence crockery is 19th century and made at the Gien factory in Orleans. The tea glasses are Moroccan, and the red wine glasses came from Sweden.*

Table linen

From as early as the 15th century, there has been a strong association between good table linen and a "civilized" household. Thus in the grander 15th- and 16th-century houses refectory tables were usually covered with various fabrics, often swagged around the sides.

During the 17th century, it was normal practice in richer homes to have a table-carpet, such as a Persian, Turkish or turkey work rug, covered during mealtimes with a washable white linen over-cloth. Such cloths, and their accompanying linen napkins, could be either plain or finely embroidered and elaborately bordered.

During the course of the 18th century, silk and printed cottons, in addition to linen, were used increasingly. By the early 19th century, striped, plaid and check cotton gingham also became fashionable, particularly in more informal settings. "Fitted" linen or cotton loose covers, to protect sideboards as well as dining tables, were also much in evidence by the 1830s. Stamped woollen velvet was a popular fabric in formal dining-rooms.

During the Victorian era, the table-carpet enjoyed a revival and Oriental-style runners were produced specifically for the purpose. Apart from linen, fashionable alternatives included velvet tablecloths with applied "panes" or bands (often gold lace), and braided borders and fringing. Hand-stitched and machine-made lace covers and mats were in vogue, especially on parlour tables and during the summer.

Above & Top: *In many areas of central France, it is still possible to purchase good examples of 19th- and early 20th-century linen tablecloths and napkins quite inexpensively. These examples were found in the Lot et Garonne region.*

Far left & Left: *A Natchez silver ladle (made by George Macpherson c.1850), and a Victorian claret jug and glasses, sit on hand-made lace tablemats from the same period.*

Top: *Moroccan tea glasses and 19th-century silver teaspoons on a 19th-century French linen tablecloth.*

Above: *A selection of Victorian table linen and cutlery in the kitchen of a French château.*

Above right: *Collections of Victorian table linen and British Royal memorabilia for sale in a shop in Los Angeles.*

Above left & Left: *A 19th-century French striped floral-pattern quilt has been utilized as a tablecloth in the courtyard of a medieval manoir in the Lot et Garonne region of central France.*

Decorative tablecloths

During previous centuries, the use of fabric covers for tables was not confined to the dining room. For example, the convention of draping dressing tables with silk and linen, ribbons and flowers, began in the Rococo interiors of France during the early 18th century. This practice was still in vogue by the end of the 19th century, but by then the cloths were usually lavishly draped muslin or calico.

Occasional tables were also often covered with a wide range of fabrics, notably Turkish and Persian rugs, embroidered linen, stamped woollen velvet, and hand-blocked or machine-printed chintzes. Paisley shawls and appliquéd or patchwork quilts were also pressed into service – particularly during the Victorian era.

In many instances, most of the above fabrics were given an additional covering of hand-stitched or machine-made lace – although lace was often used on its own where the underlying table was of sufficient quality to merit not being entirely covered up.

Top left & Below: *Early 20th-century French linen: hand-embroidered above and machine-stitched below.*

Above left: *An 18th-century toile de Jouy table cover.*

Far left: *An early 20th-century, crocheted linen mat.*

Middle left: *A modern machine-embroidered linen throw.*

Left: *An early 20th-century linen cloth, hand-embroidered in the colours of the French flag.*

Right & Top right: *A table in the drawing-room of a French manoir, covered with machine-made lace and a Victorian chenille cloth.*

Below & Middle right: *A late 19th-century French "boutie" or quilt covers a bedroom table in a 17th-century château.*

Bottom right: *A late 19th-century Russian quilt on a hallway table in a French manoir. The walls are covered in "Peony" fabric, by Bennison.*

Cushions

During the Middle Ages, large cushions or pillows were often placed on floors for the ladies of the household to sit upon. Although this form of seating has survived to the present day, notably in the use of beanbags, the primary purpose of cushions or pillows in the intervening period has been to lend additional comfort to more substantial forms of seating.

For example, in the 16th century, stools and the wooden seats of chairs were softened by the insertion of small squab cushions. Similarly, from the 17th century onward, tie-on squabs were used on French and English cane dining chairs, Gustavian furniture and rush-seated Dutch chairs. The pursuance of comfort even resulted in prototype air-cushions (containing pigs bladders filled with air) in the second half of the 18th century. In the mid-19th century, India-rubber air-cushions were used.

In addition to their functional purpose, cushions or pillows have also made a significant decorative contribution to the furnishing of interiors. For example, in the 17th and 18th centuries, they were filled with down, covered in colourful tapestries, damasks and velvets and then embellished with elaborate trimmings. These designs were symbols of both luxury and status. During the 19th century, major improvements in comfort were made to upholstered furniture by the perfection of springing and the inclusion of ever-thicker layers of stuffing and padding. However, cushions or pillows remainded popular as fashionable accessories and were used in ever greater numbers.

Above: *A piece of 19th-century English embroidered linen used to cover cushions in a French hunting lodge.*

Far left & Left: *A pillow cover of royal-purple silk surrounding a 19th-century woven Aubusson panel from an 1830s townhouse in Charleston, South Carolina, USA.*

Below: *A 19th-century French embroidered silk cushion.*

Top left: *A piece of 19th-century Aubusson tapestry weave, made into a cover with deep, bell-tassel fringing.*

Above left: *Specialist fabric manufacturers have been making artificially aged linens and chintzes for some time. They provide an authentic-looking alternative where original period fabrics are unavailable or very expensive.*

Above & Above right: *A 19th-century painted wicker bench in the hallway of a medieval French manoir. The coverlet is early 19th-century French toile. The covers are fragments of late-18th and early 19th-century toile.*

Right: *A heavy, silk damask sofa cover (in classical style), and modern velvet and silk cushions.*

1

2

3

4

5

6

1 *Covers made from kelims and other tribal rugs.*

2 *A Victorian beadwork cushion, its colours relatively unaffected by exposure to light and the passage of time.*

3 *A collection of appliqué and patchwork cushions on top of a small "Log Cabin" quilt. The red and white pillow on the left is "Single Irish Chain" pattern.*

4 *A late 19th-century floral tapestry cover.*

5 *A 19th-century cushion or pillow embellished with hand-embroidered sentimental motifs typical of the Victorian age.*

6 *A late 19th-century, hand-stitched and appliquéd round cushion on a buttoned squab covered with a 20th-century copy of a 19th-century Carreaux du Perigord fabric.*

7 *An "Old Suits" quilt and a wool-embroidered pillow.*

8 *A tapestry-covered stool and a 19th-century cushion with appliquéd flowers.*

9 *A velvet squab with a printed cotton panel, plus a printed cotton and a hand-woven tapestry design.*

10 *A Victorian Berlin woolwork cushion or pillow.*

7

10

8 9

141

Decorative details

In the 17th century, many Dutch fireplaces were dressed with detachable linen pelmets (*tours de cheminées*) attached to the underside of the smoke hood. Used to deflect smoke away from the room and up the chimney flue, they were the forerunner of the Victorian mantel frill or chimney cloth. Fashionable during the 1870s, these were almost purely decorative and made from a range of fabrics – most notably velvet, embroidered linen and lace.

Such decoration, however, was not confined to the mantelshelf. The edges of shelves and tables were similarly embellished during the Victorian era, following a decorative convention that began in the 18th century.

The introduction of electric lighting during the 1880s facilitated a further use for fabrics. Lampshades, usually with decorative fringing, began to appear in a variety of shapes and styles for chandeliers, wall and table lamps. Parchment, plain silk, silk damask and even lace looked most effective when back-lit.

Since the 18th century, fabrics have also served as decoration on fire-screens and as portable draught excluders and room dividers. Tripod-based pole screens featured tapestry, painted or embroidered silk, and raised plush and wool-worked panels – either square, rectangular or shield-shape. Many such panels were made from the needlework produced by ladies of a household during their leisure hours. Various folding panel screens were similarly embellished, although many were also made of painted, gilded or embossed leather.

Above: *A modern vellum lampshade embellished with silk braid and deep tassel fringing.*

Below left: *A modern striped-silk shade with braid edging along with silk and glass-ball fringing.*

Below middle: *Machine-made 19th-century lace has been re-used on this lampshade and a frill has been added.*

Below: *An elaborate late 19th-century gilt chandelier with pleated silk and deep-fringed shades.*

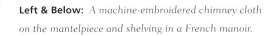

Left & Below: *A machine-embroidered chimney cloth on the mantelpiece and shelving in a French manoir.*

Bottom left: *Tasselled braid embellishing is shown on the edge of the shelves in a linen cupboard.*

Bottom right: *A "Gypsy Art" beadwork panel provides decorative edging around a Victorian tripod table.*

143

Above left & Above: *A 19th-century tri-fold, embroidered silk panelled fire-screen basks in the salon of a medieval manoir in the Lot et Garonne, France.*

Left & Far left: *A Victorian shield-shape wool and beaded fire-screen in the Monmouth Mansion, in Natchez, Mississippi, USA. The majority of screens of this type were framed and mounted on a wooden tripod to become "pole" screens. However, here, the screen is hung from a decorative brass rail that extends from a telescopic arm secured to the mantelshelf of the marble fire-surround.*

Right & Far right: *A late 19th-century five-panel tri-fold fabric screen, decorated with hunting scenes, in the salon of a medieval manoir on the Dordogne, France. The walls of the salon retain their original painted "boiserie" panelling.*

Below: *A 19th-century tri-fold gilt screen with fabric and glass panels. Such screens were primarily used as room-dividers, the glass ensuring an adequate supply of light.*

Basic techniques

The projects in this book involve quite basic sewing skills which are explained in this section. It is essential to have a large, flat surface on which to cut out fabric. A good-sized dining or kitchen table could be used; protect the surface with newspaper, a blanket or board. Avoid cutting out on the floor, particularly if it is carpeted.

BASIC SEWING KIT

◆ Scissors: a sharp pair of cutting-out shears (with slightly curved handles), a medium-sized pair of dress-makers' scissors and a pair of embroidery scissors.
◆ Pinking shears: useful for neatening raw edges.
◆ Wooden yard or metre stick: invaluable when working with large amounts of fabric.
◆ Metal or wooden ruler: useful for smaller work.
◆ Tape measure: one with a stiffened end is crucial.
◆ Retractable 5- or 7-yard metre rule: helpful for measuring up very large windows.
◆ Tailor's chalk: ideal for making easy-to-remove marks on fabric; different colours are available.
◆ Steel dressmaking pins: they won't mark the fabric. Glass-headed pins in several colours are useful when working on dark or heavily patterned fabrics.
◆ Needles: bodkins for threading, large darning needles and assorted sizes for general work. For machine sewing, keep a stock of needles of assorted types and sizes (these change according to the type of fabric you are sewing or the foot that you are using).
◆ Thimble: metal one to protect your middle finger for hand sewing, particularly for heavy fabrics.
◆ Basting cotton.
◆ Threads: synthetic thread for sewing synthetic fabrics; cotton thread for cotton and linen thread for

linen. Avoid using synthetic threads on natural fibres or cotton threads on synthetic fabrics as this may cause the work to pucker. If you are working with silk try to use a silk thread or a natural fibre thread. For general use and for medium-weight fabrics choose a medium-weight thread. For voiles, sheers, nets, muslins and other fine fabrics use a lighter gauge thread. Choose strong threads for heavy-weight fabric. Colour-match threads and fabric. For a patterned cloth match the thread to the most dominant colour and choose a tone darker than the fabric as it will appear lighter when stitched.

◆ Touch-and-close tape: two strips of tape, one with a hooked side and one with a fuzzy side that key together. Available in different widths; one type has one side of the tape stitched onto fabric, with the other stuck to a hard surface such as a cornice board so that fabric may be removed for laundering.
◆ A seam ripper: a small tool used for unpicking seams and stitches quickly.
◆ Weight: for preventing heavy or slippery fabric from sliding off the cutting table.
◆ A sewing machine: an electric or hand machine is required for most projects in this book.

SEWING BY HAND

Even though many modern sewing machines can produce an array of stitches there are times when hand sewing is necessary. For instance, before machining a seam you should baste by hand to hold the fabric firmly in position. And often the only way to achieve a really neat finish is to sew by hand. The following hand stitches will come in useful when making all sorts of soft furnishings.

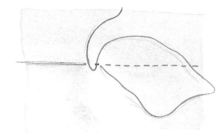

Running stitch method

This stitch consists of small, neat stitches of equal length which are made on both sides of the fabric. To pull running stitches into a gather: begin on the right side of the fabric and wind plenty of thread around a pin at the starting point to hold it. Make a line of stitches, passing the needle through from back to front of the work and finish by winding the thread around a second pin. Pull the threads by applying even pressure from each end to gather the fabric. Basting is sewn in a similar way, but with longer stitches on the working side and smaller ones on the reverse.

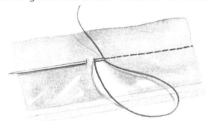

Back stitch method

A short, strong stitch, back stitch may be used instead of machining on seams or for small, difficult areas. Take a stitch backward and insert the needle at the end of the previous stitch; bring the needle under the stitch you have just made and out an equal distance in front of the thread. Repeat back and forth until you have completed a line of firm stitching.

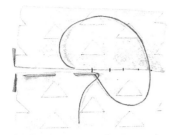

Slipstitch method

Use slipstitch to hold two folded edges of fabric together, for example on mitred corners or to attach trimmings and linings. Work on the right side of the fabric, from right to left. Place the two folded edges parallel to each other. Slip the needle inside one fold and secure the thread with a couple of back stitches. Take a small stitch inside the folded edge, sliding the needle along inside the fold for 0.75cm (¼in). Bring the needle out and catch a couple of threads from the opposite piece of fabric; continue in the same way.

Hemming stitch method

Hand hemming produces a much neater finish than hemming by machine. Work on the wrong side of the fabric, with the folded edge facing you, pointing the needle diagonally from right to left. Pick up just a couple of threads from the back of your work. Bring the needle under the folded edge and up through the fabric. If the fabric is very heavy, turn the hem over once and neaten the raw edge by adding straight binding or use herringbone stitch.

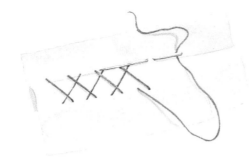

Herringbone stitch method

Otherwise known as catch stitch, herringbone is a flat stitch used instead of hemming on a raw edge. It is useful for bulky or heavy fabrics and curved hems and is employed to join overlapping edges of interlining or buckram. Work on the wrong side of the fabric from left to right. With the needle pointing right to left take a horizontal stitch through the flat layer of fabric, picking up just a couple of threads. Move the needle to the right and take a diagonal stitch again, right to left, through the edge of the folded fabric. Continue working the thread diagonally from right to left, making cross stitches across the hem edge.

SEWING BY MACHINE

Before you begin any type of machine seaming, check that the grain of the fabric is straight by pulling a thread across the width. If a pattern has been printed askew, return the fabric to the supplier before cutting out. With many fabrics it is wise to remove the selvages before seaming as they may pucker and spoil the look of the seam. As an alternative, you can cut notches into the selvage every few centimetres or inches once the seam is made, to prevent puckering.

Always stitch down the length of a seam, from top to bottom. If you are using a pile fabric such as velvet make sure that the nap (the direction in which the pile lies) runs the same way on both sides of the seam or the join will be obvious. With a very heavy pile, trim the pile within the seam allowance before stitching and ease any caught pile out of the seam with the point of a pin or a needle. If working with fine fabrics such as nets, sheers, muslin or voile use a fine-gauge needle and a suitable thread. Such fabrics tend to slip when stitching; to prevent this place tissue paper in between the two layers and sew through the paper. Tear away the paper after you have finished sewing.

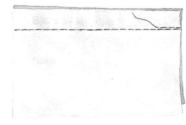

Flat seam method

To make a flat seam, first pin two pieces of fabric, matching any pattern, right sides together. Place the pins at right angles to the raw edges. Next baste down the seam line 1.5cm (⅝in) in from the raw edge; remove the pins. Machine-stitch alongside the basting, securing the seam at both ends with a few reverse stitches. Open the seam and press flat, unless you want to neaten it first or you want the bulk of the seam to lie in one direction. The simplest way to neaten a seam is to machine a row of zigzag stitches along the raw edge of the fabric. If the fabric is not liable to fray, pinking is a quick and easy solution. Fine fabrics can be turned under in a narrow fold and hemmed by hand. If the fabric is bulky, you can bind the edges with straight seam binding.

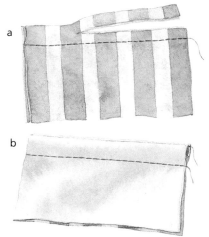

French seam method

For a totally enclosed finish with no lines of stitching showing on the right side of the fabric use a French seam. This is a very hard-wearing seam and is useful for joining fabrics when the seam will not be concealed by a lining. With wrong sides together and raw edges aligned, stitch a flat seam approximately 0.75cm (¼in) in from the open edge and trim the seam allowances slightly to reduce the bulk (a). Press. Turn the fabric back on itself so the right sides are facing and the seam lies on the fold. Baste the two layers together about 1.25cm (½in) below the seam line. Machine a second seam parallel to the first just above the basting line to enclose the raw edges (b). Remove the basting stitches. Press and turn the seam to the wrong side and the fabric right side out.

BINDING AND PIPING

Bias and straight binding can be purchased but these are usually narrow in width and light in weight and so are only suitable for edging smaller items. Piping is made by covering a purchased piping cord with bias strips of fabric and then stitching it into a flat seam.

Cord is available in different thicknesses, so choose the size according to the scale of the item you wish to pipe. Shrink cotton cord before use or it will cause the piping to pucker during washing. Boil the cord in clean water for five minutes – allow to dry before use. Always choose a fabric for binding or piping which is similar in type and weight to the main fabric. Make sure that it is shrink-resistant and colour-fast.

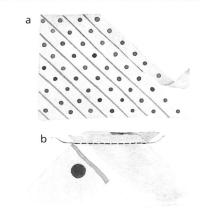

Bias strips of fabric are more flexible and have more "give". To find the true bias of a piece of fabric, fold a straight raw edge back parallel to the selvage to form a triangle of fabric – the base of the triangle is the true bias and is called the bias line. Mark out strips parallel to the bias line with a long ruler and tailor's chalk or a marker pen and cut them out, according to the width you require (a). The most usual width is 3.75cm (1½in). To make the bias binding, join the strip to give a continuous length. To do this, place two strips together at right angles to each other with right sides facing; this will form a triangle (b). Pin and machine firmly across the width, leaving a 0.75cm (¼in) seam allowance. Open out flat and press. Trim the corners to lie flat with the bias strip.

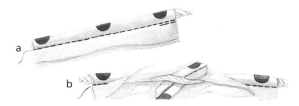

To cover piping cord, join enough bias strips together to make the required amount of piping. The binding must be wide enough to cover the cord and leave a 1.25cm (½in) seam allowance on both sides. Press the bias strip flat and place it right side down; position the piping cord in the middle and wrap the bias strip around it with wrong sides facing enclosing the cord. Baste close to the cord but do not catch it. Machine-stitch using a piping or zipper foot, or use firm back stitch if you are sewing by hand (a). Remove the basting. To join the cord, unravel two ends of cord and trim the strands to varying lengths. Overlap the ends of the strands by about 2.5cm (1in) and intertwine them so that they mesh to make a smooth join. Wrap the binding around the cord and stitch as before (b).

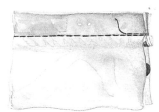

To sew the piping into the seam, place the main fabric wrong side down and lay the piped cord on top of it so that the raw edges align. Baste together. Place the second piece of main fabric right side down over the top of the piped cord, making sure that the raw edges are aligning; baste. Use a piping or zipper foot to machine the four layers together along the seamline. Remove the basting stitches.

You can neaten a raw edge with bias binding, attaching it by hand or by machine. Ready-made bias binding has pre-folded edges. If you are making your own binding turn in a narrow edge to the wrong side along both long edges and press.

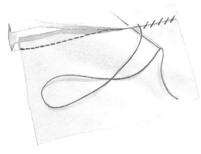

To sew by hand, open one folded edge of the binding strip. Match this to the raw edge of the fabric to be bound with right sides together. Pin and back-stitch together down the fold line of the binding. Refold the binding and turn over onto the wrong side of the fabric to be bound, enclosing the raw edge. Pin in place and hem the second folded edge of the binding to the fabric, following the first line of stitching.

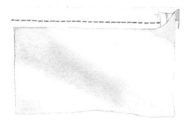

To neaten a raw edge with binding by machine, fold the binding down the middle and place wrong side down over the raw edge of the fabric to be bound. Press, baste and machine-stitch through the fabric and both folds close to the edge of the binding. Remove the basting stitches.

MEASURING UP WINDOWS

For accurate measuring use a good-quality tape measure and a steel ruler or a wooden yard or metre stick; an old fabric tape measure may have stretched so it might be less accurate. Refer to the illustration on page 150 for how to take essential measurements and note them all down on a sketch of your window. When purchasing fabric take the annotated sketch with you – this will enable the retailer to advise you on correct quantities. It does help to have someone to assist you when measuring, to hold one end of the ruler and to double-check the measurements.

Drapes or curtains

The amount of wallspace available will affect your choice of treatment so take into account the wall space when you make your original measurements. Drapes need space to stack back against the wall so that they don't block out light from the window when open, and to prevent light escaping between the drape and the wall or window when drawn. If no wallspace is available a shade or blind would be a better choice. If there is wallspace on one side only then a single drape caught to one side is appropriate.

For measuring up drapes it is preferable to have the track or pole already in position, or to know at least how wide you want it and where exactly you plan to site it. The two measurements required for calculating fabric quantity are the width and the drop. For the width measurement: when using a track the complete track length should be measured and at least 10cm (4in) added to each side for the returns. (Each return allows the drape to lie flush against the wall and hides the screws and fittings that support

the track system.) When using a track that overlaps in the middle, add an additional 7.5cm (3in) to each drape. If the drapes are to hang from a pole measure the pole length excluding the finials.

Once you have the width measurement you will need to decide on how many widths of fabric you require. As a general rule allow twice the finished width for average fullness, one and a half times for less fullness and two and a half times for fuller drapes. Multiply the number of widths of fabric by the total drop (see below) of both drapes to calculate the amount of fabric.

The drop measurement depends on the type and style of heading you plan to use and whether the drapes are to hang from a pole or a track. Decide whether the heading should hang level with, just above or just below the pole or track and calculate accordingly. Measure the drop from the top of the track, pole or window frame to the sill; then measure to the floor. Take these measurements as an extra check, even if you know you are going to have a floor-length or sill-length treatment, or if you plan to have the fabric bunching on the floor. Drapes that flap midway between the sill and floor look untidy, but sometimes, if there is a radiator under the window which does not quite come up to sill height, you may want to finish the drapes to line up with the top of the radiator. In this instance, measure from the top of the track to the top of the radiator. Also when taking initial measurements consider the flooring. If this is not yet installed, bear in mind that a thick carpet or raised flooring can make a considerable difference. Take final measurements after the floor has been laid. When measuring up drapes you will need to make allowances for hems and turnings. It is always wise to have a fairly deep hem – for example 15-20cm (5-8in) – which can be weighted to make the drapes hang better. A generous hem will also allow for any shrinkage. Allow 2.5-5cm (1-2in) for the turn-over at the top. Add these allowances to the drop.

When measuring up for a patterned fabric, take into account the repeat measurements on the manufacturer's label, or measure this for yourself. The pattern will have to be matched when the widths are joined together. This is achieved by dividing the cut drop measurement by the pattern repeat measurement and rounding it up to a whole number of repeats. Each cut drop must be made up of complete patterns. Each width cut will now be identical in pattern so the widths will match when they are joined together. The hem is an important part of the drape, so it is a good idea to choose which part of the fabric will fall at the bottom. In general, it is the pattern that will decide the hem line and it is preferable to have a row of whole motifs in the design at the bottom edge rather than a row of incomplete ones. To make sure that you can choose which part of the pattern will fall at the bottom, buy one extra pattern repeat of fabric.

Shades or Blinds

If the window is deeply recessed and has a wide reveal it is usual to position the shade or blind as close to the glass as possible. A Roman shade or blind is usually fixed on a wooden batten screwed into the underside of the top reveal. For the drop, measure from the top of the batten position to the sill and add at least 4in (10cm) for turning at the top and hemming at the bottom. (On a window frame which

is not recessed, the batten will have to be mounted on supports above the window, so increasing the drop.) For the width, measure from one side of the reveal to the other and add an extra 2in (5cm) for side hems. If the fabric is stiffened and will not fray the side hems are not necessary.

If the window is not recessed, the shade or blind will have to be mounted on the window frame if possible, or just outside it; so you should take the measurements accordingly. If there is no suitable flat part, the wood batten or roller for a roller shade or blind will have to be mounted on the wall above the frame. The wood batten, mounted track or roller may be screwed to two or more small pieces of wood in order to project far enough beyond the window to pull down easily and clear the frame.

Top Treatments

The positioning of the track, pole or cornice or pelmet board is crucial to the success of a window treatment. When measuring up, you should not only measure the window but also take the measurement from the top of the window architrave to the moulding or cornice or the ceiling itself to see how much headroom you have. Also measure the height of the top third of the window to see how much light you would lose with a cornice or pelmet. If you would lose a lot of light you should consider a different treatment.

Cornices or pelmet boards have to be fixed at the top of the window in order to conceal the track. They are usually positioned about 5-8cm (2-3½in) above the top of the window frame and project at least 5cm (2in) either side of the track to allow for end-stops and drape fullness.

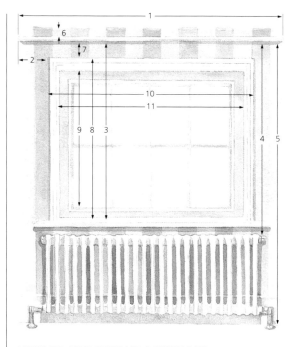

HOW TO MEASURE UP A WINDOW

Take note of all the following measurements when planning drapes or curtains and shades or blinds.

1 **Length of drape fixture**
2 **Stack back (extension of fixture beyond the window)**
3 **Drop from fixture to sill**
4 **Drop from fixture to radiator**
5 **Drop from fixture to floor**
6 **Distance from fixture to ceiling**
7 **Distance from fixture to top of window**
8 **Height or depth of window (with no recess)**
9 **Height or depth of window (inside recess)**
10 **Width of window (with no recess)**
11 **Width of window (inside recess)**

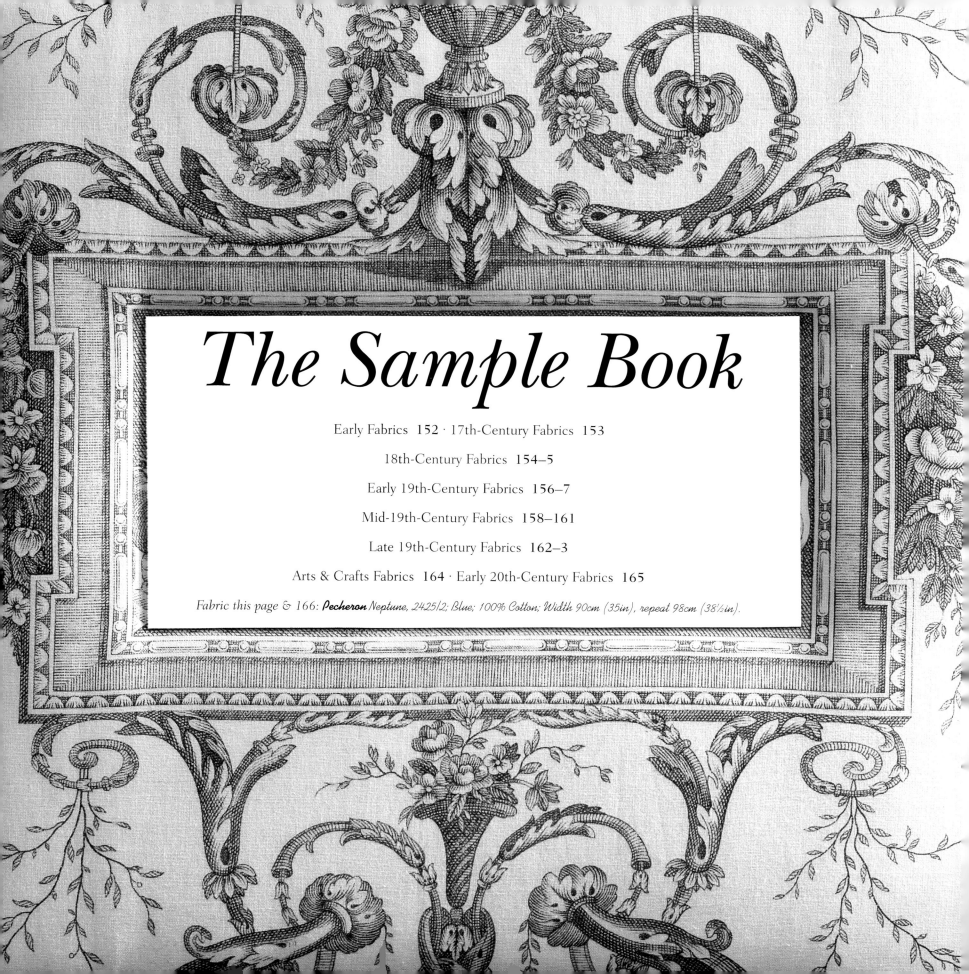

The Sample Book

Early Fabrics 152 · 17th-Century Fabrics 153

18th-Century Fabrics 154–5

Early 19th-Century Fabrics 156–7

Mid-19th-Century Fabrics 158–161

Late 19th-Century Fabrics 162–3

Arts & Crafts Fabrics 164 · Early 20th-Century Fabrics 165

*Fabric this page & 166: **Pecheron** Neptune, 2425/2; Blue; 100% Cotton; Width 90cm (35in), repeat 98cm (38½in).*

Brunschwig & Fils *C'era Una Volta,* 50984.01; Sage; 100% Cotton; Width 142cm (56in), repeat 89cm (35in).

Ian Mankin *Curtain Union;* 70% Linen, 30% Cotton; Width 145cm (57in).

Ian Mankin *Herringbone Union;* 42% Linen, 58% Cotton; Width 140cm (55in).

Monkwell *Westbourne,* M74943; Old gold 6; 100% Cotton; Width 137cm (54in), repeat 74cm (29in).

Context Weavers *Hughenden;* Petrol, Silk and Wool.

Brunschwig & Fils *Palio,* 79821.04; Rosso; 54% Linen, 46% Cotton; Width 137cm (54in), repeat 46cm (18in).

Wemyss Houlès *Montespan,* 32460; 9384 and Montespan, 33101; 9384.

Monkwell *Calcot Weaves,* M75178; Cream 2; 62% Cotton, 38% Modacrylic; Width 137cm (54in), repeat 13cm (5in).

152

17th-Century Fabrics

Brunschwig & Fils Torsade Flamestitch, 79531.G7; 51% Linen, 49% Cotton; Width 137cm (54in), repeat 64cm (25¼in).

The Gainsborough Silk Weaving Co Ltd Italian, 730011; Red; 85% Cotton, 15% Viscose; Width 127cm (50in), repeat 72cm (28in).

Sahco Hesslein Rodrigo, 08083; Blue/beige; 60% Cotton, 40% Viscose; Width 130cm (51¼in), repeat 53cm (20in)

Wendy Cushing Trimmings No. 22, Wool and silk hand-woven dot braid

Sahco Hesslein Lillian, 08886; 57% Linen, 43% Cotton; Width 140cm (55in), repeat 70cm (27½in).

Nice Irma's Handwoven Fabric Kashmir Jacobean; Multi; 100% Cotton; Width 137cm (54in), repeat 124.5cm (49in).

Parkertex Dean Fri, U1229-14; Multi; 66% Cotton, 34% Modacrylic; Width 140cm (55in), repeat 42cm (16½in).

155

18th-Century Fabrics

Jason D'Souza Fontainebleau, F3; Burgundy; 64% Linen, 36% Cotton; Width 117cm (46in), repeat 37cm (14½in).

Context Weavers Caroline B; Crimson; Silk.

Monkwell Woburn, M74995; Rose 5; 70% Viscose, 30% Modacrylic; Width 137cm (54in), repeat 28cm (11in).

G P & J Baker Capponi, J0164-35; Red; 100% Silk; Width 140cm (55in). repeat 29cm (11½in).

Zoffany Ltd Mansfield, RB366; Cerise; 100% Glazed Cotton; Width 137cm (54in).

Wendy Cushing Trimmings Special braid made to order and No. 20. Tabby braid with lays.

Jason D'Souza Le Fond, LF8; Stone; 64% Linen, 36% Cotton; Width 137cm (54in), repeat 3cm (1¼in).

Turnell & Gigon Ltd Rigodon, AB13219; Red/cream; 100% Cotton; Width 149cm (58½in), repeat 77cm (30in).

Brunschwig & Fils Pekin, 62552.01; Blue; 100% Cotton; Width 132cm (52in), repeat 36cm (14in).

Lee Jofa Buckingham Toile, LJ929004; Scarlet; 100% Cotton; Width 87.5cm (34¼in), repeat 86.5cm (34in).

Warner Fabrics Indian, CS7870; Multi on ecru; 63% Flax, 28% Cotton, 9% Nylon; Width 122cm (48in), repeat 56cm (22in).

Brunschwig & Fils Chrysso Damask, 63991.01; Currant/celadon/berry; 51% Linen, 49% Cotton; Width 147cm (58in), repeat 15cm (5⅞in).

The Gainsborough Silk Weaving Co. Ltd. S6854; Gold/yellow; 100% Silk; Width 127cm (50in), repeat 68cm (26¾in).

Warner Fabrics Audley, GP63290; Blue on cream; 100% Cotton; With 137cm (54in), repeat 2cm (¾in).

Jason D'Souza Vicomte, V71; Blue; 64% Linen, 36% Cotton; Width 118cm (46in), repeat 5cm (2in).

155

Early 19th-Century Fabrics

Zoffany Ltd Butterflies, AP0702; White; 100% Cotton; Width 133cm (52½in), repeat 48cm (19in).

G P & J Baker Panther, 257-290; Cream/black; 86% Cotton, 14% Polyester; Width 138cm (54½in), repeat 38cm (15in).

Design Archives Beaudelaire, DA 51013; Black 93; 56% Viscose, 44% Polyester; Width 140cm (55in), repeat 32cm (12½in).

Ian Mankin Empire I, Rust/neutral; 100% Cotton; Width 140cm (55in).

Design Archives Zola, DA51014; Red 12; 56% Viscose, 44% Polyester; Width 140cm (55in), repeat 23cm (9in).

Wemyss Houles Sultane, 33379, 9387

Turnell & Gigon Ltd Cesari, 45091.23; Gold; 68% Viscose, 32% Silk; Width 130cm (51¼in), repeat 20cm (8in).

V V Rouleaux Black Bonaparte 3; 87 and Blue Bonaparte 9; 86.

Zoffany Ltd Cherubs, AP0404; Blue; 52% Linen, 36% Cotton; 12% Nylon; Width 137cm (54in), repeat 118cm (46¼in).

Warner Fabrics Little Acorns, CS336080; Petrol/buff; 100% Cotton; Width 137cm (54in), repeat 10cm (4in).

Pecheron Toinette, 15398/2; Blue/yellow; 100% Cotton; Width 130cm (51¼in), repeat 124cm (48½in).

Wemyss Houlès Sultane, 33379; 910

Zoffany Ltd Bee, AW0103; Blue; 50% Modacrylic, 38% Cotton, 12% Nylon; Width 140cm (55in), repeat 8cm (3¼in).

Design Archive Hugo Stripe, DA51015; Yellow 4; 56% Viscose, 44% Polyester; Width 140cm (55in), repeat 33cm (13in).

Osborne & Little Silk Plaids, 9300/05; 100% Silk, Width 127cm (50in).

Warner Fabrics Montpelier Chintz, CS4190; Blue Ribbon; 100% Cotton; Width 137cm (54in), repeat 44cm (17¼in).

Ramm, Son & Crocker Ltd Izmir, E9621; Pink; 100% Cotton; Width 140cm (55in), repeat 64cm (25¼in).

Ramm, Son & Crocker Ltd Bagatelle, E8048; Blue/peach; 100% Cotton; Width 140cm (55in), repeat 23cm (9in).

Lee Jofa Kingsworthy, LJ929070; Eggshell; 100% Linen; Width 132cm (52in), repeat 50cm (19¾in).

Ramm, Son & Crocker Ltd Eastleigh, E2347; Red; 100% Cotton; Width 140cm (55in), repeat 101cm (39¾in).

Schumacher Pagode Chinoise, 168441; White/multi; 100% Cotton; Width 137cm (54in), repeat 64cm (25¼in).

V V Rouleaux Art 7354; 11.

Peter Jones Braid
685/46013.

Design Archives Gothic Lattice, 54035-003;
Green; 100% Glazed cotton; Width 137cm
(54in), repeat 36cm (14in).

Monkwell Verona, DA54086; Blue 2; 88% Cotton, 12%
Polyester; Width 137cm (54in), repeat 15cm (6in).

Lee Jofa Moire Rose, LJ899080;
Pink/green/cream; 100% Glazed cotton;
Width 135cm (53in), repeat 65cm (25½in).

Ramm, Son & Crocker Ltd Oakley, 65252; Blue; 52% Linen,
36% Cotton, 12% Nylon; Width 140cm (55on),
repeat 25cm (9¾in).

Ramm, Son & Crocker Ltd Blackberry,
E8075; Red/gold/cream; 100% Cotton;
Width 140cm (55in), repeat 15cm (6in).

Zoffany Ltd Indienne, AP0201; Stone;
100% Cotton; Width 133cm (52¼in),
repeat 132cm (52in).

Brunschwig & Fils Juniper Striped
Tapestry, 32821.01; Red/cream; 92% Cotton,
8% Viscose; Width 135cm (53in),
repeat 40cm (15¾in).

Peter Jones Upholstery button, 23640.

Brunschwig & Fils Kapli Stripe, 50602.01; Baltic Blues; 100% Cotton; Width 137cm (54in), repeat 30cm (11¾in).

Brunschwig & Fils St. Lucia, 36640.01; Multi; 100% Cotton; Width 137cm (54in), repeat 31cm (12¼in).

Brunschwig & Fils Cavaillon, 32433.01; Yellow; 77% Viscose, 23% Cotton; Width 140cm (55in), repeat 8cm (3¼in).

Context Weavers Penrhyn; Terracotta; Silk and Cotton.

Design Archives Ribbon Trellis, DA54073; Blue 2; 100% Cotton; Width 137cm (54in), repeat 50cm (19¾in).

Ramm, Son & Crocker Ltd Mae East, E9070; Green; 100% Cotton; Width 140cm (55in), repeat 50cm (19¾in).

160

Schumacher Oatland's Plantation Toile,
167861; Red; 56% Linen, 33% Cotton, 11% Nylon;
Width 137cm (54in), repeat 46cm (18in).

Schumacher Williamsburg Parrots and
Blossoms, 168214; Document brick; 100%
Cotton; Width 137cm (54in), repeat 32cm (12in).

Brunschwig & Fils Chinese Leopard Toile, 79.280.04; Multi;
100% Cotton; Width 137cm (54in), repeat 40cm (15½in).

Ramm, Son & Crocker Ltd Belgravia, J2010;
Green; 46% Velicren, 29% Cotton,
16% Linen, 9% Nylon;
Width 140cm (55in), repeat 3.5cm (1⅜in).

Schumacher Pagode Chinois, 168444; Yellow/green;
100% Cotton; Width 137cm (54in), repeat 64cm (25¼in).

Wendy Cushinh Trimmings (Above) No. 21; Tabby braid with lays and cord twist: (Below) No. 23, Conso Shella

V V Rouleaux Braid 4725; 1312

Late 19th-Century Fabrics

Monkwell Murano, MQ5373; Red 4; 52% Cotton, 48% Modacrylic; Width 137cm (54in).

Laura Ashley Mr. Jones, 057489; Navy/ burgundy/sand; 100% Cotton; Width 122cm (48in), repeat 5cm (2in).

Watts Montagu Cut Ruche, Seaweed, 70007-06/N9; Kenya Red, 7007-05/N9.

Parkertex Vienna, VO190-495; Red; 100% Cotton; Width 140cm (55in).

Parkertex Thessaloniki, C7092-12; White; 95% Cotton, 5% Polyester; Width 150cm (59in), repeat 60cm (23½in).

Monkwell Arona, MQ5375; Black/gold 1; 52% Cotton, 48% Modacrylic; Width 137cm (54in), repeat 40cm (15¾in).

Context Weavers Belton; Parchment Silk

V V Rouleaux
Tassels from braid
no. 1811.

Ramm, Son & Crocker Ltd Surrey, E9133; Pink/green/ black;
100% Glazed cotton; Width 140cm (55in), repeat 63cm (24¾in).

Monkwell Empoli, M75374; Green 12;
52% Cotton, 48% Modacrylic;
Width 137cm (54in), repeat 2cm (¾in).

Charles Hammond Swinburne,
HAC4037; Multi; 100% Cotton; Width
140cm (55in), repeat 35.5cm (14in).

**Wendy Cushing
Trimmings**
No. 24, Tapestry
braid, custom-made.

Watts Montagu Diced Picot
Braid, Seaweed, 70006-06/149;
Kenya Red, 70006-05/109.

Arts and Crafts Fabrics

Liberty Ianthe, 1095022-E; Multi; 53% Linen; 35% Cotton; 12% Nylon; Width 137cm (54in), repeat 31cm (12in).

Monkwell Welcome Home, MQ5355-4; 41% Polyester, 34% Polypropylene, 25% Cotton; Width 137cm (54in), repeat 36cm (14in).

Sanderson Willow Bough Minor, PR7676/1; Blue/green/cream; 100% Cotton; Width 137cm (54in), repeat 23cm (9in).

Liberty Hera, 1475002A; Multi; 36% Modacrylic, 33% Cotton, 25% Polyester, 6% Polypropylene; Width 137cm (54in), repeat 54cm (21¼in).

Monkwell Vine, MQ5223-10; 100% Cotton; Width 137cm (54in), repeat 31cm (12in).

Liberty Briarwood, 1067024-A; Red/green/cream; 100% Cotton; Width 138cm (58¼in), repeat 20cm (8in).

Liberty Braids, Range 88; 220001; from left to right L, N & M.

V V Rouleaux 3.221/23; 30

Early 20th Century Fabrics

Parkertex Tiberius, M1609705; 37% Polyester, 25% Cotton, 24% Modacrylic, 14% Viscose; Width 138cm (54¼in), repeat 21cm (8¼in).

Monkwell Seedpod, M75221-7; 100% Cotton; Width 137cm (54in), repeat 8cm (3¼in).

Warner Fabrics Aquarium, CS7900; Orange; 100% Cotton; Width 137cm (54in), repeat 72cm (28¼in).

Firifiss Murano, FF74031–3; 100% Cotton; Width 152cm (59¾in), repeat 61cm (24in).

Monkwell Criss Cross, M75222-7; 100% Cotton; Width 137cm (54in), repeat 5cm (2in).

Firifiss Merino, FF71006-8; 100% Wool; Width 137cm (54in), repeat 15cm (6in).

G P & J Baker Gallery, J0242230; 100% Silk; Width 140cm (55in), repeat 18cm (7in).

Firifiss Cheviot, 71012-006; 100% Wool; Width 137cm (54in), repeat 7cm (2¼in).

Ramm, Son & Crocker Ltd Abingdon, E8189; Light green; 100% Cotton; Width 140cm (55in), repeat 41cm (16in).

165

Directory

FABRIC SUPPLIERS

The fabrics featured can be obtained internationally, either via a distributor or store, or by mail order. Write to the first address given for your nearest stockist. In some cases there are a number of distributors; contact the head office address provided for details. Distributors often supply the fabrics of a number of manufacturers. In such cases you will only find the name of the distributor under the manufacturer's entry. You will need to refer to the distributor, listed alphabetically in this directory, for the address. (Telephone numbers are not included as they change frequently.)

Alexander Beauchamp
Vulcan House
Stratton Road
Gloucester
GL1 4HL
England

Alton-Brooke
5 Sleaford Street
London SW8 5AB
England

Andrew Martin Ltd
200 Walton Street
London SW3 2JL
England

USA distributor
Kravett & Travers Inc

Anna French Ltd
108 Shakespeare Road
London SE24 0QW
England

USA distributor
Classic Revivals

Anta Scotland Ltd
Fearn
Tain
Ross-shire
IV20 1XW
Scotland

Arthur Sanderson & Sons Ltd
100 Acres
Oxford Road
Uxbridge
Middlesex UB8 1HY
England

UK showroom
112–120 Brompton Road
London SW3 1JJ
England

Available in USA at
D & D Building
979 Third Avenue
New York NY 10022

Baer and Ingram
273 Wandsworth Bridge
 Road
London SW6 2TX
England

Baker Knapp & Tubbs Inc
917 Merchandise Mart
Chicago Ill.60654
USA

G P & J Baker Ltd
West End Road
High Wycombe
Bucks HP11 2QD
England

USA distributor
Lee Jofa

Beaumont & Fletcher
98 Waterford Road
London SW6 2HA
England

Bennett Silks
Crown Royal Park
Higher Hillgate
Stockport SK1 3HB
England

Bennison Fabrics
16 Holbein Place
London SW1W 8NL
England

Available in USA at
76 Greene Street
Soho
New York NY 10012

Bergamo Fabrics
37-20 34th Street
Long Island City
New York 11101
USA

Bery Designs
157 St. John's Hill
London SW11 1TQ
England

Borderline Fabrics
1 Munro Terrace
London SW10 0DL
England

Boussac Tissu D'Ameublement Ltd
27 rue du Mail
75002 Paris
France

Available in UK at
8 The Quadrangle
49 Atalanta Street
London SW6 6TU
England

Beaumont & Fletcher

Available in USA at
979 Third Avenue
New York NY 10022

Brian Yates
Riverside Park
Caton Road
Lancaster LA1 3PE
England

Brunschwig & Fils
D & D Building
979 Third Avenue
New York NY 10022
USA

Available in UK at
10 The Chambers
Chelsea Harbour Design
 Centre
London SW10 0XE
England

Charles Hammond
27 Chelsea Harbour
 Design Centre
London SW10 0XE
England

Charles Koenig Associates
Hornbeam
Dorney Wood Road
Burnham
Bucks SL1 8EH
England

Chelsea of London Ltd
Cranford House
Springvale Terrace
London W14 0AE
England

Chelsea Textiles
7 Walton Street
London SW3 2JD
England

Christopher Norman Inc
979 Third Avenue
16th Floor
New York NY 10022
USA

UK distributor
Charles Koenig Assoc.

Clarence House
211 58th Street
New York NY 10022
USA

Classic Revivals
1 Design Center Place
Boston
Mass. 02210
USA

Cole & Son Ltd
144 Offord Road
London N1 1NS
England

Colefax and Fowler
118 Garratt Lane
London SW18 4DJ
England

USA distributor
Cowan & Tout

Context Weavers
Park Mill
Holcombe Road
Helmshore
Rossendale
Lancs BB4 4NP
England

Cowan & Tout
D & D Building
979 Third Avenue
New York
NY 10022
USA

The Decorative Fabrics Gallery
278–280 Brompton Road
London SW3 2AS
England

Decorator's Walk
171 East 56th Street
New York
NY 10022
USA

De Le Cuona Designs
1 Trinity Place
Windsor
Berkshire SL4 3AP
England

The Design Archives
P.O. Box 1464
Bournemouth
Dorset BH4 9YQ
England

USA distributor
Classic Revivals

Designers Guild
3 Olaf Street
London W11 4BE
England

Available in France at
Osborne & Little
10 rue Saint-Nicolas
75012 Paris

Donghia
23 Chelsea Harbour
 Design Centre
London SW10 0XE
England

Elizabeth Eaton
85 Bourne Street
London
SW1N 8HF
England

Fabricut
9303 East 46th Street
Tulsa OK 74145
USA

Firifiss Contemporary Textiles
P O Box 1464
Bournemouth
Dorset BH4 9YQ
England

USA distributor
Lee Jofa

Gallery of Antique Costume & Textiles
2 Church Street
London NW8 8ED
England

The Gainsborough Silk Weaving Co Ltd
Alexandra Road
Sudbury
Suffolk CO10 6XH
England

George Smith
587–9 King's Road
London SW6 2EH
England

George Spencer
4 West Halkin Street
London SW1X 8JA
England

Greeff Fabrics
200 Garden City Plaza
Garden City
New York
NY 11530
USA

Groves Bros. Fabrics
5084 Brush Creek Road
Fort Worth
Texas 76119
USA

UK distributor
Charles Koenig Assoc

Henry Newbery & Co Ltd
18 Newman Street
London W1P 4AB
England

Hill & Knowles
13 Mount Road
Feltham
Middlesex TW13 6AR
England

Hodsoll McKenzie
52 Pimlico Road
London SW1W 8LP
England

Ian Mankin
109 Regent's Park Road
London NW1 8UR
England

Ian Sanderson Ltd
PO Box 148
Newbury
Berkshire RG15 9DW
England

Jab International Furnishings Ltd
1/15–16 Chelsea Harbour
  Design Centre
London SW10 0XE
England

Jagtar
6 rue Vivienne
75002 Paris
France

Available in UK at
22 Chelsea Harbour
  Design Centre
London SW10 0XE
England

Jane Churchill
Colefax and Fowler

USA distributor
Cowan & Tout

Jason D'Souza Ltd
42 Queensland Road
London N7 7AH
England

John Boyd Textiles Ltd
Higher Flax Mills
Castle Cary
Somerset BA7 7DY
England

John Stefanidis
261 Fulham Road
London SW3 6HY
England

Kravett & Travers Inc
225 Central
Avenue South
Bethpage
Long Island
New York NY 11714
USA

UK distributor
Andrew Martin Ltd

Laura Ashley
27 Bagleys Lane
London SW6 2BW
England

Available in USA at
6 St. James Avenue
Floor 10
Boston MA 02116

Lee Jofa
D & D Building
979 Third Avenue
New York NY 10022
USA

Available in UK at
19 Chelsea Harbour
Design Centre
London SW10 0XF
England

Lelievre
13 rue du Mail
75002 Paris
France

Available in UK at
101 Cleveland Street
London W1P 5PN
England

USA distributor
Stark Carpets/O.W.W.

Lennox Money
93 Pimlico Road
London SW1W 8PH
England

Lewis & Wood
12 Westcroft Square
London W6 0TB
England

Liberty Furnishings
3 Chelsea Harbour
Design Centre
London SW10 0XE
England

USA distributor
Ramm Son & Crocker

The Malabar Cotton Company
The Coach House
Bakery Place
119 Altenburg Gardens
London SW11 1JQ
England

Manuel Canovas Ltd
125 rue de la Faifanderie
75116 Paris
France

Available in UK at
2 North Terrace
Brompton Road
London SW3 2BA
England

Available in USA at
979 Third Avenue
New York NY 10022

Marvic Textiles Ltd
1 Westpoint Trading
  Estates
Alliance Road
London W3 0RA
England

UK showroom
12–14 Mortimer Street
London W1N 7RD
England

Available in France at
5 rue du Mail
75002 Paris

Available in USA at
979 Third Avenue
Suite 1502
New York NY 10022

Mikhail Pietranek
Saint Swithan Street
Aberdeen AB1 6X
Scotland

USA distributor
Cowan & Tout

Monkwell
10-12 Wharfdale Road
Bournemouth
Dorset BH4 9BT
England

USA distributor
Lee Jofa

Mulberry Home Collection
76 Chelsea Manor Street
London SW3 5QE
England

Nice Irma's Handwoven Fabric
46 Goodge Street
London W1P 1FJ
England

Nina Campbell
UK distributor
Osborne & Little

Nobilis-Fontan Ltd
29 rue Bonaparte
75006 Paris
France

Available in UK at
1/2 Cedar Studios
45 Glebe Place
London SW3 5JE
England

Available in USA at
57A Industrial Road
Berkeley Heights NJ 07922

Nouveau
54–8 Queens Road
Doncaster
South Yorkshire DN1 2NH
England

Old World Weavers Fabrics
D & D Building
979 Third Avenue
New York NY 10022
USA

Osborne & Little
49 Temperley Road
London SW12 8QE
England

Available in USA at
Suite 520N
979 Third Avenue
New York 10022

Pallu & Lake
27 Chelsea Harbour
  Design Centre
London SW10 0XE
England

USA distributor
Lee Jofa

Parkertex
West End Road
High Wycombe
Bucks HP11 2QD
England

USA distributor
Lee Jofa

Percheron
6 Chelsea Harbour
  Design Centre
London SW10 0XE
England

Pierre Deux
870 Madison Avenue
New York NY 10021
USA

Pierre Frey
47 rue des Petits Champs
75001 Paris
France

Available in UK at
253 Fulham Road
London SW3 6HY
England

Ralph Lauren
2 Place de la Madeleine
75008 Paris
France

Available in UK at
143 New Bond Street
London W1Y 9FD
England

Available in USA at
867 Madison Avenue
New York
NY 10021

Ramm, Son & Crocker
Chiltern House
Gordon Road
High Wycombe
Buckinghamshire
HP13 6EQ
England

Available in USA at
200 Clearbrook Road
Elmsford NY 10523

V V Rouleaux Ltd
10 Symons Street
Sloane Avenue
London SW3 2TJ
England

Rubelli
Palazzo Corner
 Spinelli
San Marco
3877 Venice
Italy

Available in France at
6 bis rue de L'Abbaye
76006 Paris

UK distributor
Percheron

Sahco Hesslein UK Ltd
24 Chelsea Harbour
 Design Centre
London SW10 0XE
England

USA distributor
Bergamo Fabrics

Scalamandré
300 Trade Zone Drive
Ronkonkoma
New York 11779-7381
USA

UK distributor
Altfield
G4 & 2/22 Chelsea
 Harbour Design Centre
London SW10 0XE

Schumacher
939 Third Avenue
New York NY 10022
USA

UK distributor
Turnell & Gigon

Souleiado
39 rue Proudhom BP21
13151 Tarascon Cedex
France

Stark Carpets/O.W.W
979 Third Avenue
New York
NY 10022
USA

Stroheim & Romann
155 East 56th Street
New York
NY 10022
USA

**Stuart Renaissance
Textiles**
Barrington Court
Nr Illminster
Somerset TA19 0NQ
England

Tassel Time
1249 Stirling Road
Dept HBED1
Dania
FL 33004
USA

Timney Fowler
388 King's Road
London SW3 5UZ
England

Tissunique Ltd
2–10 Chelsea Harbour
 Design Centre
London SW10 0XE
England

Titley & Marr
141 Station Road
Liss
Hampshire GU33 7AJ
England

Today Interiors Ltd
Hollis Road
Grantham
Lincolnshire NG31 7QH
England

Turnell & Gigon Ltd
20 Chelsea Harbour
 Design Centre
London SW10 0XE
England

Warner Fabrics
Bradbourne Drive
Hillbrook
Milton Keynes
MK7 8DE
England

UK showroom
9 Chelsea Harbour
 Design Centre
London SW10 0XE
England

Watts of Westminster
2/9 Chelsea Harbour
 Design Centre
London SW10 0XE
England

Wemyss Houlès
40 Newman Street
London W1P 3PA
England

**Wendy Cushing
Trimmings**
G7 Chelsea Harbour
 Design Centre
London SW10 0XE
England

Available in USA at
261 Fifth Avenue
Suite 1001
New York NY 10016

Whittaker & Woods
5100 Highlands Parkway
Smyrna
Georgia 30082
USA

**Williamsons Inc
Documentary Fabrics**
The Copper Lantern Inc
248 Sound Beach Avenue
Old Greenwich
CT 06870-1626
USA

**Zimmer & Rohde
UK Ltd**
15 Chelsea Harbour
 Design Centre
London SW10 0XE
England

Available in USA at
41 East 11th Street
9th Floor
New York NY 10003

Zoffany
Talbot House
17 Church Street
Rickmansworth
Hertfordshire WD3 1DE
England

Distributed in USA by
Whittaker & Woods

Zuber
28 rue Zuber
68170 Rixheim
France

Available in UK at
42 Pimlico Road
London SW1W 8LP
England

Available in USA at
D & D Building
979 Third Avenue
New York NY 10022

HOUSES OPEN TO THE PUBLIC

*The following historic houses have fine collections
of period soft furnishings which have either been
photographed for the book or referred to in the text
as important to the history of soft furnishings.*

UK

Abbotsford House
Melrose
Roxburghshire
Scotland

The American Museum
in Britain
Claverton Manor
Bath
Avon
England

Aston Hall
Aston Park
Trinity Road
Aston
Birmingham
England

Burghley House
Stamford
Lincs
England

Castle Ward
Srangford
Co. Durham
N Ireland

18 Folgate Street
Spitalfields
London
England
By appointment

The Geffrye Museum
Kingsland Road
London
England

The Georgian House
7 Charlotte Square
Edinburgh
Scotland

**The Georgian
House**
7 Great
 George Street
Bristol
Avon
England

Hagley Hall
Hagley
Near Stourbridge
West Midlands
England

Hopetoun House
South Queensferry
West Lothian
Scotland

Lanhydrock
Bodmin
Cornwall
England

Leeds Castle
Leeds
Kent
England

Leighton House
12 Holland Park Road
Londo
England

**Linley Sambourne
House**
18 Stafford Terrace
London
England

Mellerstain House
Mellerstain
Gordon
Berwickshire
Scotland

Osborne House
York Avenue
East Cowes
Isle of Wight
England

Parham House
Pulborough
West Sussex
England

Plas Newydd
Llanfairpwll
Anglesey
Gwynedd
Wales

Preston Manor
Preston Park
Brighton
Sussex
England

Number 1 Royal Crescent
Bath
Avon
England

The Royal Pavilion
Brighton
East Sussex
England

The Vyne
Sherborne St. John
Basingstoke
Hampshire
England

Wellington Museum
Apsley House
149 Piccadilly
London W1
England

Wightwick Manor
Wightwick Bank
Wolverhampton
West Midlands
England

USA

Adirondack Museum
Blue Moutain Lake
New York 12812

Andrew Low House
329 Abercorn Street
Savannah
Georgia 31401

Atlanta Historic Society
3101 Andrews Drive NW
Atlanta
Georgia 30305
Two historic houses
Tullie Smith House
and **The Swan House**

Bartow Pell Mansion
Shore Road
Pelham Bay Park
Bronx NY 10464

Belle of the Bends
508 Klein Street
Vicksburg
Mississippi 39180
Historic guest house

The Belvedere Mansion
1008 Park Avenue
Galena
Illinois 61036

Boone Hall Plantation
Highway 17N
Charleston
SC 29403

The Briars
31 Irving Lane
Natchez MS 39120
Bed & breakfast inn

The Burn
712 N Union Street
Natchez MS 39120
Bed & breakfast inn

Cedar Grove
2300 Washington Street
Vicksburg
Mississippi 39180
Historic inn

The Charleston Museum
360 Meeting Street
Charleston
SC 29403

Davenport House Museum
324 E State Street
Savannah
Georgia 31401

Dezoya House
1203 Third Street
Galena
Illinois 61036
Historic guest house

Drayton Hall
3380 Ashley River Road
Charleston SC 29414

Edmonston-Alston House
Ashley River Road
Charleston SC 29414

The Garth Woodside Mansion
RR1 Hannibal
Missouri 63401
Bed and breakfast inn

Gloucester
201 Lower Woodville
   Road
Natchez MS 39120

Green Leaves
303 South Rankin Street
Natchez MS 39121

The Guest House
201 N. Pearl Street
Natchez MS 39120
Bed and breakfast inn

Heyward-Washington House
87 Church Street
Charleston SC29414

Joseph Manigault House
350 Meeting Street
Charleston SC 29414

Juliette Gordon Low Birthplace
142 Bull Street
Savannah
Georgia 31401

Lansdowne
1323 Martin Luther King
   Road
Natchez MS 39121

Manship House
420 E Fortification Street
Jackson
MS 39202-2340

Melrose
Natchez National
   Historical Park
Melrose Avenue
Natchez MS 39121

Monmouth
36 Melrose Avenue
John A Quitman
   Highway
Natchez MS 39121
Historical inn

Morris Jumel Mansion
West 160th and
Edgecombe Avenue
New York NY10032

Natchez Pilgrimage Tours
Canal at State Street
P.O. Box 347
Natchez MS 39121
*Houses open for the
Natchez Spring & Fall
Pilgrimage Tours*

Nathaniel Russell House
51 Meeting Street
Charleston SC 29401

Old Merchants House
29 East 4th Street
New York NY 10003

Owens Thomas House
124 Abercorn Street
Savannah
Georgia 31401

Rosalie
Corner Canal and Orleans
Streets
Natchez MS 39121

Sands Willet House
366 Port Washington
   Boulevard
Port Washington
New York NY 11050

Telfair Academy of Arts & Sciences
121 Barnard Street
Savannah
Georgia 31401

Thomas Elfe House
54 Queen Street
Charleston SC29401

Waverley
West Point
Nr. Columbus
Mississippi 39773.

Glossary

a

Acanthus: Ornamental foliage based on the leaves of a Mediterranean plant. Used in Classical, Byzantine, Romanesque and Gothic architecture, and popular as a decorative motif on fabrics since the Renaissance.

Aesop's fables: Classical tales or narratives involving animals and birds, and intended as moral instruction. Popular in illustrated European literature from the 15th century onward, they provided a source of inspiration for fabric designs well into the 20th century.

Aesthetic Movement: A decorative style that began in Britain in the 1860s as a reaction to the "over-industrialized" ornamental products of the Victorian era. Overlapped with the Arts and Crafts Movement.

Aniline dyes: Synthetic dyes produced from coal-tar. Developed in the late 1820s, but not in common use until the late 1850s.

Appliqué: The technique of applying cut-out pieces of fabric on top of a base cloth.

Arts and Crafts Movement: A movement initiated primarily by William Morris in Britain in the late 19th century, and devoted to a return to traditional methods of craftsmanship and design. It was a reaction to the industrialization of craftsmanship.

Aubusson: Carpets and tapestries produced from c.1665 in the "Royal Manufactory" at Aubusson, in France. They employed two methods of weaving: thick pile carpets on vertical high warp looms, as at Savonnerie; close or short pile carpets, using the tapestry technique, on horizontal low warp looms.

Axminster: The town in Devon, England, in which Thomas Whitty established a carpet factory in 1755. Prior to 1860 the factory produced hand-woven, woollen pile carpets (known as Axminster carpets); thereafter machine-made equivalents were also produced. The factory moved to Wilton, England, in 1835.

b

Baronial style: Mock-Gothic style of architecture and decoration based on medieval ecclesiastical designs. Popular during the late 19th century.

Baroque style: An ornate style of architecture and decoration associated with 17th-century Italian architecture. Characterized by an abundant use of cupids, cornucopias and similar motifs set in symmetrical, curvaceous designs.

Battenburg lace: Handmade lace produced in Battenburg, a village in western Germany.

Beauvais: A city in northern France reknowned since the Middle Ages for its production of fine-quality tapestries.

Berlin woolwork: Canvas embroidery worked in worsted yarns. Originated in Germany; particularly popular during the 1840s.

Bobbin: A wooden, bone or glass reel or spool used for winding and weighting yarn.

Bobbin lace: A lace worked with thread wound on bobbins. Patterns are produced by entwining threads around pins pierced into a pillow or cushion.

Boiserie: Originally wood panelling decorated with carvings in shallow relief. Also refers to fabrics embellished with raised patterns stitched in relief.

Bolster: A long pillow, usually cylindrical in shape.

Bourette: A silk fabric in plain weave with a rough, knotty surface.

Boutie: Traditional French quilt.

Braid: Woven ribbon of almost any fibre (including metallic threads) used for trimming and edging.

Brocade: A heavy fabric in which elaborately figured patterns are raised against a ground cloth by the addition of supplementary wefts. Traditionally made of silk or cotton, but nowadays can be made from any fibre.

Brocatelle: A woven fabric with two warps, which produced slightly raised designs. Mostly in satin against a plain ground.

Brussels carpet: Loop-pile carpeting, usually of two or three colours, but sometimes more.

Buckram: Coarse, stiffened cotton or linen and used to line pelmets or cornices.

Bullion fringe: Thick fringing made of twisted loops of rope, in either silk, wool or metallic threads.

Burlap: Coarse canvas made of jute.

Byzantine: Styles of architecture, design and decoration common to the Byzantine Empire (founded 395AD after partition from the Roman Empire) and, in particular, Constantinople. Combined forms borrowed from Graeco-Roman classicism with oriental motifs from Arab countries. Typical ornamentation included vines, swans, peacocks, palmettes, geometrical patterns, colourful mosaics and the Tree of Life.

c

Calico: A plain-weave cotton fabric, generally cream coloured. Originally from India, but also printed in the West from the 17th century onward.

Cambric: Firm, fine, plain-woven cotton.

Camlet: A plain-woven ribbed cloth in which different yarns are often combined with worsted.

Campaign chair: A folding chair, originally designed for ease of transportation during military campaigns.

Canapé: An ornate style of French settee.

Canonball bed: A style of bed in which the four corner posts are topped with (usually wooden) cannonball-shaped cappings.

Cappings: The usually decorative tops of objects such as posts, rods and poles, but also the top, cap-like covering of any fixture or fitting.

Castellated: A form of decoration, in which a wall or any fixture or fitting is alternatively raised and indented (usually along its top edge) in the style of battlements. Also known as crenellation.

Charles Eastlake: A 19th-century (1836–1906) architect and writer and critic on and of the arts. His publication *Hints on Household Taste in Furniture, Upholstery and other Details* was first published in London in 1858, and in America in 1872. Enormously influential, particularly in America, it was reprinted many times. Containing a mixture of his own designs and other leading architects of the day, it provided an important link between the Victorian Gothic revival and the Arts and Crafts Movement. In America his designs for architecture and interiors became known as 'Eastlake Style'.

Chenille: A fabric with a velvety pile, originally made from wool or cotton but now also from synthetic fibres.

Chinoiserie: Western adaptations of Oriental and Chinese designs and patterns.

Chintz: Plain-woven printed cotton cloth, traditionally printed with flowers or birds and usually glazed, popular in the 18th century.

Classical: Styles of architecture, decoration and designs founded in Ancient Greece and Rome.

Classical revivals: Adaptations of the above styles during the 15th- and 16th-century Renaissance, the 17th-century Baroque period, 18th-century Palladianism and early-19th-century classical revivals.

Colonial style: A term used to describe North American architecture and decoration, from the early 17th century to the creation of federal government in 1789.

Composition: An amalgam made from paper or wood pulp, plus whiting and glue. It was primarily used to make applied decorative mouldings.

Cornice: Either a decorative moulding at the top of the wall, just below the ceiling, or a valance-like device above window drapes.

Cotton: A natural fibre from the boll (the fruit) of the cotton plant, spun and woven into fabric.

Cotton gin: A machine for separating the seeds from the fibre of cotton.

Counterpane: A coverlet for a bed.

Crazy quilt: A patchwork quilt in which the individual patches of material are of different sizes, shapes, colours and fabrics: the whole forming an irregular-shaped pattern.

Cretonne: Unglazed chintz.

Crewelwork: Outline embroidery, stitched in wool on linen or linen mixtures.

Crochet: Decorative work consisting of intertwined loops, executed in wool, cotton or silk thread with a small hook.

Cut-pile velvet: A type of velvet in which the warp threads are lifted over metal wires or strips to form loops, which are then cut to form a dense, short pile.

d

Damask: Self-patterned fabric made of silk, cotton or linen on a jacquard loom, mixing shiny and dull yarns.

Dimity: A ridged cotton fabric made from double or triple yarns.

Dobby: An attachment for a loom that produces small geometric patterns.

Dornix: A cloth of linen warp and woollen weft, usually with largish patterns.

Drawboy loom: Originated in the Near East and best known for the production of figured silks; a forerunner of the jacquard loom.

Dress curtains: The primary hangings in a window display. They are often fixed open (and cannot be pulled shut) – the light being controlled by secondary drapes, sheers, blinds or shutters.

Duncan Phyfe: An American furniture maker (1768–1854). Born in Scotland, he settled in New York where he produced designs based on the English Regency and French Empire styles.

e

Embroidery: Decorative surface stitching.

Empire style: A style of architecture and decoration popular in France c.1804–30, and the United States c.1810–30. Incorporated Classical and Egyptian motifs.

f

Face cloth: Term used for the main fabric of a drape.

Fäience: Glazed coloured earthenware.

Farthingale: A 17th-century chair that was armless and had a seat wide enough to accommodate females wearing voluminous skirts known as "farthingales".

Federal style: A style of architecture, furniture and decoration fashionable from the early years of American independence (1789–1830). Incorporated many patriotic and military symbols, such as the eagle.

Festoon: Either a window drape fixed at the top of the window and drawn up in one piece (on cords) to form a swag, or a garland tied together with ribbons and suspended between two points so that it drapes.

Field: The area of a wall above the dado and below the cornice.

Fillet: A moulding, usually of gilded wood, used as a trim for wall coverings.

Finials: Decorative ornaments on the ends of spires, pinnacles, gables, posts and rods. From a purely practical point of view, they stop curtain rings falling off the ends of curtain poles. Originally of carved, cast or moulded foliage, but also of numerous other decorative forms ranging from acorns to pagodas.

Flame stitch: A form of decorative stitching in which the basic pattern mimics the narrow, triangular shape of flickering flames.

Four-leaf clover bed: 19th-century, American term for a four-poster bed – also known as a "four apostle" bed.

Furbelow: A gathered or ruffled piece of fabric.

Fustian: A coarse cotton and linen twill with a nap.

g

Galloon: A decorative tape or ribbon.

Gaufrage: An embossed surface created by compressing fabric between heated plates or rollers.

Genoese silk: Silk fabrics made in the Italian city of Genoa.

Georgian style: An 18th-century style of architecture, furniture and decoration characterized by the proportions and ornaments of Classical architecture.

Gingham: A cotton fabric, usually woven in white with one other colour to create the characteristic checked or striped pattern.

Goblet pleating: A heading for drapes featuring fat "goblet" shaped pleats in which the tubes of "goblets" are filled with wadding, batting or a contrasting coloured fabric for definition.

Gothic revival: A 19th-century revival of the original Gothic style of architecture and decoration which flourished between the 11th and 15th century.

Gothick: An 18th- and early 19th-century spelling of Gothic; denotes the delicate applied ornament fashionable before the full-scale Gothic revival.

Gypsy art: Decorative work, usually stitched, produced by travellers and itinerant craftsmen.

Ground cloth: The base fabric or material on to which other fabrics or decorative stitchings are applied.

Greek revival: A strand of Neo-classicism, based on Ancient Greek forms, that played a major role in European and American design from c.1750–1850.

Gustavian style: A Swedish style of architecture and decoration based on Neo-classical style and developed during the reign of Gustave III in the last quarter of the 18th century. Characterized by symmetry, straight lines, restrained ornamentation and elegance.

Gustav Stickley: Hugely influential American furniture-maker (1857–1942) who worked out of Syracuse, New York, USA. As editor of the *Craftsman* magazine he propagated the ideas of the Arts and Crafts Movement throughout America.

h

Hand-blocking: The technique of stamping patterns and motifs onto cloth using wood or metal blocks.

Harateen: A worsted furnishing material.

Hemp: A coarse fibre derived from plants and used to make rope.

Holland: A fine-quality linen cloth.

Huguenots: A French protestant religious community, who specialized in weaving and lace-making. To escape religious persecution at the end of the 17th century, they emigrated in large numbers to other European countries, notably England and Switzerland, where they created thriving textile industries.

i

Interlining: Material sewn between the main fabric and the lining to give strength, stiffen or add body.

Inverted pleat: This is formed like a box pleat in reverse so that the edges of the pleats meet to conceal the extra fabric at the back.

j

Jacquard loom: Combines the harness mechanism of a drawloom with a punch-card system (rather like a piano roll) which mechanically selects the warp threads and raises them when necessary. Produces an elaborately figured reversible woven fabric.

Jacobean: Architecture and decoration characteristic of the reign of James I of England (1603–25).

Jute: A bast fibre often used for burlap or twine.

k

Kelim: A pileless ethnic wool, cotton or silk rug woven like a tapestry, and characterized by narrow slits between blocks of colour.

l

Lace: Light open-work fabric made from cotton, worked by either hand or machine.

Lambrequin: A stiff, shaped surround that goes across the top of a window, like a pelmet or cornice, but then continues down the sides.

Lampas: A figured weave in which extra wefts and warps are used to add further colour and pattern in addition to those formed by the main warp and weft.

Lawn: A delicate, lightweight fabric (like cambric), usually made of cotton but can be linen or polyester.

Linen: Fabric produced from the stalks of flax, a plant native to the Mediterranean and temperate climates.

Lit a la turque: A type of bed, first introduced to Europe in the 18th century, in which the bedstead was placed parallel to the wall and had a small canopy or half-tester above it supporting drapery which trailed down over each end of the bed.

Lit bateau: A French bed with outwardly curving, wooden head- and foot-boards, their shape approximating to the stern and bow of a boat.

Loom: An apparatus for weaving cloth made by interlacing yarns at right angles.

m

Manoir: The French equivalent of an English manor house.

Marquetry: A form of decorative work, usually on furniture, in which contrasting coloured materials, such as wood, ivory and metal, are inlaid on an object to form patterns and motifs.

Mesangère: Fashionable and eccentric French designer (1761–1831) who popularized Empire style in France during the early 19th century.

Mercerized: Chemical treatment of cotton fibres using caustic potash or soda to produce lustre, strength and better absorption of dyes.

Middle Ages: The historical period between the fall of the Western Roman Empire and the Renaissance (5th–15th century).

Mohair: Cloth made either wholly or in part from the high-quality soft wool of the Angora goat.

Moiré: A ribbed fabric (often taffeta) with a wavy, watered appearance produced by calendering. Watered moiré patterns can also be woven into the fabric.

Monogrammed: Items ranging from fabrics to furniture that have been decorated with the initials or symbol of either the patron or the owner. Also known as cyphering, the initials were often interwoven to form flat linear patterns across a surface.

Moquette: A woollen fabric woven by looping the warp yarn over wires which are then withdrawn to form loops that can be cut or uncut. Used for upholstery the loops can be cut or uncut.

Mordant: A chemical agent used for fixing dyes to fibres, making them colourfast and washable.

Moreen: A type of watered camlet.

Muslin: A plain-weave cotton gauze, varying in texture from fine to coarse.

n

Nap: The fibrous surface or pile of a fabric. The predominant direction of the nap affects the way in which the fabric reflects light, and therefore its apparent colour.

Napoleon III-style: 19th-century, French, ornate interiors and furniture in a style in vogue during the reign of Napoleon III.

Navajo: A Native American tribe who produced striking ethnic rugs – many of the designs being copied by European settlers for use on rugs and quilts.

Needlepoint lace: Hand-made lace produced with a needle and thread, using buttonhole stitching – as opposed to bobbin lace, which is made by twisting and entwining bobbins carrying threads around pins embedded in a pillow.

Neo-classical style: Architectural and decorative style based on the forms of Ancient Rome and Greece.

Neo-renaissance: Known also as Renaissance revival – a 19th-century movement of architecture and design, influential in both Europe and America, in which the classical ornamentation and motifs of the 16th-century Italian High Renaissance were reintroduced, particularly for grander houses and public buildings.

Nottingham lace: A machine-made lace produced in Nottingham, England. Mass-produced, it is less expensive than handmade lace and is made from coarse cotton in patterns derived from 16th-century European handmade lace.

o

Oiled floorcloth: Canvas that has been stiffened with linseed oil, and then either painted or stencilled. Used as a covering on hardwood floors instead or rugs or carpets.

Organza: Also known as Organdy. A fine, sheer plain-weave cotton fabric that can be dyed, printed or white.

Ottoman: A low, upholstered footstool or sofa.

p

Pagoda-style: Structures and motifs in the style of Eastern temples, featuring upturned leaves, fretwork brackets and decorative finials and pendants. On fabrics the motif is primarily associated with *chinoiserie* designs.

Paisley pattern: Design based on Indian (Kashmiri) patterns, notably curvilinear, highly stylized floral forms. Named after the Scottish town where shawls were made during the 19th century using fine worsted.

Palladian: An interpretation of the Classical style developed by the Italian architect Andrea Palladio (1508–80). Bought to England in the 17th century by Inigo Jones, revived in the early 18th century and influenced American architecture in the late 18th century.

Papier mâché: A lightweight material made of paper pulp and glue, which can be moulded to form decorative objects and painted.

Parchment: The treated skin of a sheep, goat or other animal. Mainly used for writing on, but also employed in the manufacture of lampshades.

Parquet: A floor covering made of wooden blocks installed in a pattern (such as herringbone).

Passementerie: Braids and trimmings.

Perigord check: A distinctive checked fabric produced designed and produced in the Perigord region of France.

Pinking shears: Scissors with zigzag edges used to prevent raw edges from fraying.

Petit-point: Close, hand-embroidered stitchwork, usually worked in tapestry wool.

Pie-crust ruffles: A frill or trim with edges that have been crimped in a similar manner to the way in which pastry is pinched or crimped around the rim of a pie.

Plaid: A twill or plain-woven cloth with a pattern of intersecting stripes in both the warp and the weft.

Plush: A soft, heavy fabric with an even pile that closely resembles velvet. Usually made of wool, but also silk and cotton, and also referred to as velour.

Portiéres: Drapes hung over the doors or doorways of a room.

Pouffe: A soft ottoman (a low, stuffed seat without a back) or large hassock (a stuffed cushion), often cylindrical in shape.

Prudent Mallard: Well-known American furniture-maker, who worked out of New Orleans during the middle of the 19th-century. Produced large, high-quality pieces.

Puddling: A decorative style in which window drapes are deliberately over-long, so that they slightly spread out, or "puddle", over the floor. Often used as a symbol of status and wealth.

r

Regency: Styles of architecture, furniture and decoration popular in England between 1811–20.

Renaissance: The flowering of Classical scholarship, scientific, artistic and geographical discovery, and the assertion of the active and secular over the religious and contemplative life after the Middle Ages.

Rep: A ribbed cloth of lightly woven cotton or wool.

Return: The side edges of a pelmet, cornice or valance that run between the front edge and the window or wall.

Reveal: The side walls of a window niche.

Rococo style: A style of architecture and decoration first popularized in France during the 1720s. Derived from *rocaille*, or shell decoration; essentially a freer, more frivolous development of Baroque style.

Rococo revival: 19th-century revival of Rococo style.

Rosette: A circular fabric "rose" used to decorate drapes, swags and tails etc.

Ruche: Gathered or pleated strip of fabric used as a trimming.

Ruffle: A strip of material gathered to form a frill.

Runner: Either a strip of cloth used as a table cover or ornament, or a narrow carpet or rug (used, for example, in a passageway or on stairs).

Rush: A grass-like plant that grows in marshy areas, the dried stalks are used for matting and seating.

S

Sarsnet: A thin, transparent silk of plain weave.

Sash window: A window with a glazed wooden frames that slides up and down in vertical grooves by means of rope cords attached to counterbalanced weights. Also known as a "double-hung" window.

Satin: A smooth, lustrous fabric (of Chinese origin) made from silk, cotton or synthetic fibres. The right side is shiny and the wrong side matte.

Say: A thin woollen fabric (or serge) of twill weave. Can also be made of silk.

Savonnerie: A French carpet factory established by Pierre Dupont in 1627 in an old soap factory (hence the name Savonnerie). By royal decree they produced elaborately thick pile carpets on large, high warp looms. Initially, all their output was for the French king and his palaces, and visiting dignitaries. Later, however, they sold to the public, and the term Savonnerie came to signify carpets made elsewhere in the style of the original factory.

Saxon blue: A blue-coloured dye purported to be based on a shade of blue used by the Germanic peoples – the Saxons – who conquered England during the 5th and 6th centuries AD.

Seigneurial: The feudal ruling classes – lords of the manor.

Sericulture: The growing of mulberry trees and the breeding of silk worms (which feed exclusively on the leaves of this tree).

Silksey-woolsey: A cloth made of silk warp and woollen weft. Linsey-woolsey has a linen warp and woollen weft.

Scotch carpet: A double-cloth ingrain carpet woven in Scotland. Ingrain refers to the fact that the yarn was dyed before weaving.

Shaker style: A simple, functional style of architecture, furniture and decoration developed by the rural North American community known as the Shakers.

Silk: A natural fibre produced by the silk worm.

Sisal: An agave fibre used for making rope and floor covering.

Smocking: Embroidery on a regular tight-pleated ground. Back-stitch or running stitch hold the pleats in place, which are then re-embroidered.

Spinning Jenny: Machine for twisting threads to strengthen, lengthen and variegate them.

Strapwork: An ornamentation of crossed, interlaced and scrolled straps resembling leather and often used on wall-hangings.

Stuffed-over: A form of upholstered seating applied to the seats of dining and occasional chairs. Either sprung or unsprung, the upholstery stuffing sits on top of webbing attached to the underside of seat frame, while the top cover fabric extends over the top and down the sides of the seat frame.

Stuffs: A term in general use up until around the end of the 19th century, used to describe various kinds of worsted cloths, including moreens and camlets.

Stumpwork: Embroidery (usually figurative) worked from figures derived from stamps or engravings.

Swags and tails: A decorative window treatment: the swags are draped horizontally; the tails vertically down either side. Swags are sometimes known as festoons.

Swiss lace: A 19th- and 20th-century, machine-made imitation of 16th-century, hand-made Swiss lace. Mostly produced in Nottingham, England, this coarse cotton lace was primarily used for sheers and window blinds or shades.

Swiss-cotton eyelet: A late-19th-century, Swiss, cut or open-patterned, machine-made type of whitework. Primarily used for curtains and drapes.

t

Tapisserie: Primarily French for tapestry, but also French for wall-hangings, upholstery and interior decoration in general.

Taffeta: A crisp, plain-weave fabric made from synthetic fibres, occasionally from silk. Originally tapestries were hand-embroidered or flat-woven.

Tapestry: Heavy woven fabric, traditionally with pictorial designs; used as wall-hangings or for upholstery.

Tartan: A woollen cloth woven to create a checked design. Individual tartan designs relate to families, places or regiments in Scotland and Ireland.

Ticking: Heavy cotton twill fabric usually in herringbone texture, used to cover pillows, squabs and mattresses. Traditionally woven with a fine stripe in black, blue, or red on white.

Toile: A "pattern" made from inexpensive fabric, used to test an effect prior to cutting out the face cloth.

Toile de Jouy: A printed cotton fabric originally made in the French town of *Jouy-en-Josas*, in 1760. Traditionally, romantic pictorial scenes are printed in one colour on a natural ground.

Tow: A type of worsted material.

Tripod table: A table with three legs.

Trog sofa: A Scandinavian settee, made of painted wood (sometimes gilded), and usually upholstered with squab cushions.

Turkey work: Heavy woven fabric or embroidery made using knots in imitation of hand-woven Persian and Turkish carpets.

Twill: A basic weave with a diagonal grain, created by floating the weft over and under several warps.

V

Valance: A soft window or bed pelmet or cornice, or a skirt around the base of a bed.

Vellum: A fine type of parchment made from calf skin.

Velour: *See* Plush.

Venetian windows: Windows or archways with three openings, the central one a wide arch, the side ones narrower and usually flat-topped. They became a hallmark of Palladian architecture in the 18th century.

Verdure: Literally means "greenness". Verdure tapestries had a predominantly green-coloured cast.

Vert de gris: The French name for a colour similar in appearance to verdigris: the blue-gray-green coating of basic cupric carbonate that forms in the atmosphere on copper, brass or bronze.

Velvet: A luxurious fabric with closely woven pile, made from cotton, silk, or synthetic fibres. Various types are available and it can be plain or patterned.

Voile: A fine crisp fabric made from silk, cotton or synthetic fibres, usually used for sheer drapes.

W

Warp: A set of fixed threads set lengthways on a loom.

Watering: A technique used for finishing cloths of plain weave, with a heavier weft than warp, to give them a watered, or waved, appearance.

Weft: The crosswise threads that are interlaced over and under the warp threads to produce a woven fabric.

White mull: A soft white cotton imported from India from the 17th century onward, but later also made in Europe, and particularly Switzerland. It can be either plain or embroidered with floral motifs, and is largely used for petticoats, trimmings and sheers.

William and Mary: English monarchs who reigned from 1688–94.

William Morris: A highly influential 19th-century (1834–96) designer, artist-craftsman, poet and author who, as the leading member of the Arts and Crafts Movement, advocated a return to traditional methods of design and construction.

Wilton: An English town which, from 1741, produced cut-pile woollen carpeting. After 1835, when the Axminster (*see* above) factory moved there, hand-knotted carpets were also produced.

Worsted: Lightweight, smooth woollen cloth made of long staple fleece which has been carded and combed to give it a strong, even-quality twist.

Index

Page numbers in *italic* refer to the illustrations

a

à la duchesse beds, 103, 114
accessories, 132-42, 132-43
Ackermann's Repository of Arts, 10, *38, 50*
Aesthetic Movement, 11, 90
air cushions, 138
Alençon, 9
America:
　carpets, 58
　chintzes, 8
　country rugs, 63
　craft revivals, 11
　drapes, 14
　four-poster beds, 103
　lace, 9
　pelmets, 20
　portières, 73
　quilts, 131
American Museum, Bath, *115*
Amish, *89,* 131
Andrew Low House, Savannah, Georgia, USA, *20, 21, 82*
angora wool, 7
aniline dyes, 89
Antwerp, 9
appliquéd cushions, *141*
appliquéd quilts, 131, 136
Arabian beds, 114
Argenton, 9
Arkwright, James, 10
armchairs:
　loose covers, 94-7, *94-7*
　upholstery, *79, 81,* 86-7, 92
Arts and Crafts Movement, 11, 90
Aubusson carpets and rugs, 10, 58, 58, *126-7*
Aubusson tapestries, 77, *138, 139*
Axminster carpets, 10, 58

b

back stitch, 146
Baronial style, 77
Baroque style, 20
basting cotton, 146
beadwork, *10,* 11, *141, 143*
Beauvais tapestries, 77
beds, 100-31
　coronas, *120-5,* 121-5
　four-poster beds, 102-3, *102-11*

beds (cont.)
　half testers, 114, *114-19,* 116-19
　quilts, *130-1,* 131
　standard beds, 126, *126-9*
bedsteads, 126
Bennison, *19, 25, 45, 137*
bias binding, 148, 149
binding, 148-9
blinds, 43
　measuring up, 150
　Roman, 16-17, *16, 17,* 150
bobbin lace, 9
Bologna, 6
bolsters, 84-5, *84-5*
Bordeaux, 10
"bouties", *8,* 130, 131, *137*
The Briars, Natchez, Mississippi, USA, *50*
brocades, 6, 8, 14, 102
brocatelle, 8, 66, 73
Brussels, 9
Brussels weave carpets, 58
Burgundy, 7, 8
The Burn, Natchez, Mississippi, USA, *24*
buttoning, 98, *98-9*

c

Calhoun Mansion, Charleston, Carolina, USA, *12-13, 33, 34-5, 52, 53, 87, 105*
calico, 136
camlet, 7
"campaign" fringes, 50
carpets, 8-9, 10, 56-61, 58
"Carreaux du Perigord" cotton, *89, 141*
Cartwright, Edmund, 10
Cedar Grove, Vicksburg, Mississippi, USA, *29, 32, 110*
chairs:
　buttoning, 98, *98-9*
　cushions, 138
　loose covers, 92, 94-7, *94-7*
　upholstery, 74-98, *74-99*
Château de Compiègne, *59*
Château du Parc, *15*
checks, upholstery, *88-9,* 89
chenille, 73
chimney cloths, 142, *143*
China, 6, 8
chinoiserie, *7*
chintz, 8, 9, 10-11, *44-5,* 45, 103, 136
Classical style, 27, 58, 77, *87*

Colefax and Fowler, 45
Constantinople, 6
"conversation settees", *74-5, 98*
Coote, Belinda, *27*
cord, piping, 148
cords and tassels, 54-5, *54-5*
cornices, 20-3, 150
coronas, *120-5,* 121-5
cotton:
　chintz, 8, 9, 10-11, *44-5,* 45, 103, 136
　drapes, *15*
　table linen, 134
"crazy" quilts, *131*
crewelwork, 9, 66, *67*
crochet, 11
Crompton, Samuel, 10
curtains:
　coronas, *120-5,* 121-5
　door curtains, *72-3,* 73
　half-testers, *114-19,* 116-19
　measuring up, 149-50
　see also drapes
cushions, 138, *138-41*

d

damasks, 6, 8, 11
　four-poster beds, 102
　portières, 73
　upholstery, *80-3,* 81
　wall-hangings, 66
day bed, squabs, 84-5, *84-5*
deep-buttoning, 98, *98-9*
Delobel, 100
documentary fabrics, 6, 11, *11, 21, 24*
door curtains, *72-3,* 73
drapes, 12-14
　edgings, 50, *50-1*
　headings, 25, *25*
　measuring up, 149-50
　poles, *18-19,* 19
　ruffle-edged, *46-9, 46-9*
　sheers, *42-3,* 43
　swags, *26-37, 27-37*
　tie-backs, 50, 52, *52-3*
dyes, 6, 10, 89

e

East India Companies, 8
Eastlake, Charles, 73, 90, 103
edgings, 50, *50-1*
Egyptian style, carpets, 58
embroidery, Opus Anglicanum, 8, 11
Empire style, 19, 27, 43, 67, 81, 87
England:
　carpets, 10
　drapes, 14
　four-poster beds, 103
　Opus Anglicanum, 8, 11

England (cont.)
　quilts, 131
　upholstery, 77, 89, 98
　woollens, 7

f

fabric samples, 151-67
Federal style:
　carpets, *61*
　four-poster beds, *111*
　pelmets, 20, *20*
　poles, 19
　swags, 27
　wall-hangings, 67
fire-screens, 142, *144*
fireplaces, 142, *143*
Flanders, 8, 9, 77
flat seams, 147
Flemish headings, 25
float-tufting, 98
floorcloths, 63
floors, carpets and rugs, 8-9, 10, *56-65,* 58, 63-5
Florence, 6, 8
"Four Apostle" beds, *107*
"four-leaf clover" beds, *107*
four-poster beds, 102-3, *102-11*
France:
　carpets, 9, 10, 58
　chintzes, 10
　drapes, 14
　lace, 9
　pelmets, 20
　silks, 6
　tablecloths, 136
　upholstery, 89
French-pleat headings, 25
French seams, 148
fringes, 50
Frost, Edward Sands, 63
fustian, 7

g

Garth Woodside Mansion, Hannibal, Missouri, USA, *114*
gaufrage velvets, 8, 90
Genoa, 6, 8, 9, 11, 90
gingham, 89, 134
Gloucester Mansion, Natchez, Mississippi, USA, *32, 39*
Gobelins tapestries, 77
Gothic revival, 20, 77, 89
Greek revival, *18, 19,* 92, *104*
Green Leaves, Natchez, Mississippi, USA, *42, 43, 51, 73, 106*
Gustavian furniture, 89, *89,* 138

h

half testers, 102, *114, 114-19,* 116-19

hand sewing, 146-7
harateen, 10
Hargreaves, James, 10
Harper, Buzz, *32*
headings, 25, *25*
Heal, F. & Son, 114
hemming stitch, 147
herringbone stitch, 147
Holland, 89, 142
hooked rugs, 63, *63,* 65
Hope, Thomas, 10
Huguenots, 8, 50

i

India, 8, 45, 89
indiennes, 8, 45
Industrial Revolution, 10, 11
Italy, 6, 7, 9, 14, 90

j

Jacobean revival, 77
Jacquard looms, 11, 81

k

Kay, John, 10
Kidderminster, 10
kilims, *141*

l

lace, 9
　machine-made, 10, 11, *11*
　sheer drapes, *42-3,* 43
　table linen, 134, *134,* 136
lambrequins, 14, 20, 38-41, *38-41,* 42
lampshades, 142, *142*
Lansdowne, Natchez, Mississippi, USA, *38*
leather:
　upholstery, 90, *90*
　wall-hangings, 66, 67
Leaver lace-making machine, 10
Leeds Castle, Kent, England, *66, 67,* 108-9
linen, 8, 10
　damask, 81
　table linen, 134, 136
　upholstery, 89
Linley Sambourne House, London, England, *73*
lits à la Turque, 120
lits bateau, 120
lits d'ange, 114, *114*
"Log Cabin" quilts, *141*
London, 8, 10
looms, 8, 10, 11, 81
loose covers, 92, 94-7, *94-7,* 134
Louis XIV, King of France, 8, 50, 100
Low Countries, 8

Lucca, 6
Lyons, 6, 8, 10, 11

m

Macpherson, George, *134*
Mallard, Prudent, *111, 115*
Manchester, 89
mantel frills, 142
Marot, Daniel, 20, 27, 73
Marseilles, 10
measuring up, 149-50
Mechlin, 9
medieval fabrics, 6-8
Melrose Mansion, Natchez, Mississippi, USA, *21, 51, 53, 82, 99*
Mesangère, *50*
Milan, 6, 9
mohair, 67
moirés, 102
Monmouth Mansion, Natchez, Mississippi, USA, *74-5, 76, 111, 115, 144*
moquette, 66
moreen, 10, 11
Morris, William, 77
Morris Jumel Mansion, New York, USA, *120*
Mortlake, 77
mosquito nets, *100,* 103, 114, 121, *121*
muslin, 11, 43, 136

n

Nantes, France 10
napkins, 134, *134*
Napoleon I, Emperor, *120*
Nathaniel Russell House, Charleston, South Carolina, USA, *38, 50, 51, 83*
Native American rugs, 63
needles, 146
needlework, 9, 142
Neo-classical style:
　carpets, 58
　swags, 27
　upholstery, 77, 81, *81, 87*
Neo-Gothic style, 39
Neo-Renaissance style, 39
Neo-Rococo style, 27, 89, 92, 99

o

Old Merchants House, New York, USA, *19*
"Old Suits" quilts, *141*
Opus Anglicanum, 8, 11
organza, *104*
Oriental carpets, *56-7,* 58
Owens Thomas House, Savannah, Georgia, *29, 82, 99*

p

paisley patterns, *8*, 136
Palermo, 6
Palladian style, 20, 81, 103
Parham House, Sussex, England, *72, 77*
Paris, 9, 10
passementerie, 14, 50, 52
patchwork, 131, 136, *141*
pattern repeats, 149-50
pelmets or cornices, 14, 19, 20-3, *20-4*, 150
   four-poster beds, *105*
   half-testers, 117
   lambrequins, 38-41, *38-41*
Pennsylvania, 131
Pennsylvanian Dutch, 63
Perigord fabric, *103*
Persian carpets and rugs, 58, *58*, 66, 134, 136
petit-point, 9, *77*
Philadelphia, 11, 58
Phyfe, Duncan, *6*
piping, 148
plaids, 89
plush, 73, 90
pole screens, 142
poles, *18-19*, 19
polonaise beds, 103, 121
portières, *72-3*, 73
Provençe, 10, *69*
Pusher lace-making machine, 10

q

quilts, *8*, 11, *15*, *100-1*, *103*, 107, *130-1*, *135*, 136, *141*

r

rag rugs, *62-5*, 63, *64-5*
Regency style:
   four-poster beds, *106*
   pelmets or cornices, 20
   poles, 19
   swags, 27
   under-curtains, 43
   upholstery, *82*, 89
   wall-hangings, 67
Renaissance, 6-8
Rhode Island, 89
Rococo style, 81, 103, 136
Roman blinds or shades, 16-17, *16*, *17*, 150
Rosalie, Natchez, Mississippi, USA, *21*, *35*, *53*
Rouen, France, 10
ruffle-edged drapes, 46-9, *46-9*
rugs:
   country rugs, *62-5*, 63-5
   formal rugs, 58
   table coverings, 134, 136
rulers, 146
runners, 134
rush matting, 63

s

sarsanet, 14
sashes, 43
satins, 6, 67
Savonnerie carpets, 10, 58, 59
say, 7
Scalamandré, *6*, 11, *20*, *29*, *82*, *99*

Schumacher, *24*
scissors, 146
"Scotch" carpet, 58
screens, 142, *144-5*
seam rippers, 146
seams, 147
   flat, 147
   French, 148
settees, *74-5*, *98*, *99*
sewing kit, 146
sewing machines, 146, 147
shades, see blinds
Shakers, 63, 132
sheers, *42-3*, 43
shelves, decorations, 142, *143*
Sheraton, Thomas, 20
shirred rugs, 63
"siamoise", 43
silks, 6, 8, 10, 11
   four-poster beds, 102, 103
   table linen, 134, 136
   under-curtains, 43
   upholstery, 80-3, 81
Singer sewing machines, 10
"Single Irish Chain" pattern, *141*
slip stitch, 147
slipcovers, 92, 94-7, *94-7*
Smith, George, *98*
smocked headings, 25, *25*
sofas, *87*, *89*, *99*
Souleiado, *69*, *73*
Spain, 6, 7
Spitalfields, London, England 10, 11
squab cushions, *98*, 138, *141*
   day beds, 84-5, *84-5*
Stickley, Gustav, 90

stitches:
   back stitch, 146
   hemming stitch, 147
   herringbone stitch, 147
   running stitch, 146
   slip stitch, 147
stripes, upholstery, *88-9*, 89
stumpwork, 9
swags-and-tails, 14, *26-37*, 27-37, *111*
Sweden, 89
synthetic dyes, 6, 10, 89

t

table-carpets, 134
table linen, 134, *134-5*
tablecloths, *132-5*, 136, *136-7*
tablemats, *134*
tables, edgings, 142, *143*
taffetas, 6, 8, 67, 102
tailor's chalk, 146
tails, 14, 30-1, *31*
tape measures, 146, 149
tapestries:
   cushion, 138, *141*
   four-poster beds, 102, *105*
   Opus Anglicanum, 8
   upholstery, 77, *77-9*
   wall-hangings, 66, 67
tartan, *63*, 89
tassels, 50, *50-1*, 52, *52-5*, 54-5
techniques, 146-50
Temple Newsam House, Leeds, *106*
tented walls and ceilings, 67
thimbles, 146
threads, 146

tie-backs, 14, 50, 52, *52-3*
toiles, *9*, 10, *14*
toiles de Jouy, 10, *69*, 131, *136*
touch-and-close tape, 146
tours de cheminées, 142
Trapunto quilting, *131*
tufting, 98
Tullie Smith House, Atlanta, Georgia, USA, *131*
turkey work, 8-9, 58, 66, 134
"Turkish" beds, 103
Turkish carpets and rugs, 58, 66, 134, 136

u

under-curtains, 43
upholstery, 74-98
   buttoning, 98, *98-9*
   checks and stripes, *88-9*, 89
   damask and silk, *80-3*, 81
   leather, 90, *90*
   styles, 92, *92-3*
   tapestry, 77, *77-9*
   velvet, 90, *90-1*, 92

v

valances, 46-9, 112
   four-posters, *105*, 112
   half-testers, 114, 116-19
velvets, 6, 8, 11
   drapes, 14
   portières, 73, *73*
   sewing, 147
   tablecloths, 134, 136
   upholstery, 90, *90-1*, 92
Venetian windows, 20, 27

Venice, Italy, 6, 9
verdure tapestries, 67, 77
Versailles, 8, 100
Victoria, Queen of England, *63*, 114
Victorian age:
   buttoning, 98
   carpets, 58
   decorative details, 142
   four-poster beds, 103
   headings, 25
   pelmets, 20
   table linen, 134, 136
   upholstery, 77, 92

w

wall-hangings, 66-7, *66-71*, 70-1
watered silk, *12-13*
Watts and Co., *30*, *84*
weights, 146
Wharton, Edith, 43
   The Decoration of Houses, 12
"Whig's Defeat" quilts, *131*
Whitney, Eli, 10
Wilton, Lord, 9-10
Wilton carpets, 10, 58
window treatments, 12-55
windows, measuring up, 149
woollens, 7-9
   carpets, 8-9, 10
Worcester, 77
worsteds, 7, 14, 66, 67, 81

y

yard sticks, 146

Acknowledgments

In addition to the houses mentioned in the Directory, the author and publishers would like to thank the following house-owners, interior designers, curators and museums;

Tim and Edda Abegg; Julian Adams, Historic Natchez Foundation; Olivia Alison, Owens Thomas House, Savannah, USA; Anta Scotland Ltd; Betty Letts Arnold, Andrew Low House, Savannah, USA; Cornelia Bayley; Kip and Alison Bertram; Robert Blackwell and Harry Gorst, Gloucester, Natchez, USA; Stephen Bohan-Davis, The Juliet Gordon Lowe House, Savannah, USA; Robert E. Canon and Newton Wilds, The Briars, Natchez, USA; Jim and Liz Cherry;

The Comoglio Showroom; Ian and Lesley Corke; Clifford Ellison; Mary Giles, Charleston Museum; Christophe Gollut, 116 Fulham Road, London SW3 6HU, England; Paul and Lisa Grist; Marguerite Guercio, Monmouth, Natchez, USA; Linda Gumb; Amelia Handegan, Interior Design, Gadsdon Street, Charleston, USA; Buzz Harper, Harper's Antiques, Toulouse Street, New Orleans, USA; Thierry and Agnes Hart; Gedney M. Howe 111, The Calhoun Mansion, Charleston, USA; Richard Jenrette; Bill Justice, National Park Centre Headquarters, Natchez, USA; Bertrand and Sophie Lalande, Chateau du Parc, Saint Ferme; Robert Leath, Historic Charleston Foundation;

John and Margaret Marshall MacIlroy, Lansdowne, Natchez, USA; Lord and Lady McAlpine; Jim and Debbie Millis; Gill and Jean Baptiste Monpezat; Yves and Raphaelle de Montvert; Virginia Beltzhoover Morrison, Green Leaves, Natchez, USA; Chris O'Connell; Tom Parr; Mike and Lynne Pemberton; Valerie Perry, The Charleston Preservation Society; Shearer K. Pettigrew, The Calhoun Mansion, Charleston, USA; Vangie Rainsford; Jacki Sadoun; Graham and Liz Sangster; Jacqueline Serres; Lars Sjoberg; The Souleiado Museum; Sally Spillane; Eric and Gloria Stewart; Stuart Interiors; The Telfair Academy of Art, Savannah; The Trustees of Leeds Castle, Kent, England; Lyn von Kirsting.